Police
Instructor

Deliver Dynamic Presentations,
Create Engaging Slides, &
Increase Active Learning

Richard H. Neil Sr.

"Do not withhold good from those who
deserve it, when it is in your power to act."
~Proverbs 3:27

Police Instructor *– Deliver Dynamic Presentations, Create Engaging Slides, & Increase Active Learning*

Copyright © 2011 *LEOtrainer LLC & Richard H. Neil Sr.*
ISBN-13: 978-1466476356   ISBN-10: 1466476354

Police Instructor is dedicated to my wife Gloria, my daughter Nadia, and my son Richard Jr. They provided me with a foundation of strength and passion throughout my career. They continue to serve as my inspiration in all things – including Police Instructor – which would not have been possible without their love and support.

I also dedicate the handbook to the law enforcement families around the globe. They must exhibit courage each day as they make sacrifices that other families will never experience. Thank God for their love and support.

Without sacrifice there can be no justice – there can be no society.

How to Use Police Instructor

Police Instructor is a collection of activities, techniques, tips, examples, scenarios, stories, and resources that will benefit any training topic in law enforcement. Whether you are teaching a class of new recruits, field training a rookie, serving as an SRO, delivering a speech to a civic group, or conducting roll-call training, you will be able to use the resources in this book to enhance their learning experience. Feel free to ignore the ideas that you don't like and change the ideas that will serve you best in a different way.

Police Instructor is also a quick reference for your classes. Use the notes area provided at the end of each chapter to record your ideas, cases, and stories for future audiences. If you run short of information, use one of the interactive exercises throughout the book to ensure that the class will remember the material that you have provided.

Let *Police Instructor* be your ally by providing you with a variety of methods to enhance your training – law enforcement and society will both benefit from your efforts.

The Disclaimer

I wrote this book for law enforcers who train law enforcers, and I am not interested in being politically correct. If you are not a law enforcer, police instructor, or someone with a real connection to the world of law enforcement, this book may offend you. It is deeply opinionated, painfully honest, and personal. If you do not like hearing the truth, this book may not be for you - I recommend you go with fiction.

I have included examples of how I do things behind the scenes and in the classroom; however, like the making of hotdogs, not everyone wants to see how it's done. You probably will not like and use every one of the suggestions, but you will find many of them compelling if you train cops or cadets.

I believe whole-heartedly that our profession will benefit from the new methods and innovative ideas provided in Police Instructor – I am confident of that – but I would not insult you or any other instructor by saying I know your audience better than you do. No one can assure you that a certain activity or technique will work every time. If someone says otherwise, they are selling you a bottle of snake oil. If a particular method does not work for you – stop using it or change it for your class.

Police Instructor – The Mission

Our mission is to improve the safety of our law enforcers and the society they serve through more effective training.

We hope that you find large helpings of knowledge and some glimpses of wisdom throughout these pages. Implement as many of the tips and techniques as you can; you will see a significant improvement in your presentations and audience participation.

Police Instructor seeks to instill these guiding principles in law enforcement educators and trainers worldwide:

* **Cops & Cadets learn better** when they are given the opportunity to talk and not forced to only listen.

* **Cops & Cadets learn better** when you present information as if you were having a conversation with a friend instead of lecturing a class.

* **Cops & Cadets learn better** when you use pictures and images on your slides and not just text and bullet points.

* **Cops & Cadets learn better** when they write down information instead of just hearing it.

* **Cops & Cadets learn better** when they are given small chunks of wisdom instead of an iceberg of information.

* **Cops & Cadets learn better** when they are moving around and not constantly sitting.

* **Cops & Cadets learn better** when they are shown how the knowledge being taught will be of value to them.

* **Cops & Cadets learn better** when they are challenged to think critically, be creative, and communicate with others.

* **Cops & Cadets learn better** when you incorporate a *variety* of techniques and create an atmosphere of active learning.

Some may not like investing the time that active methods require, but we train warriors, not scholars. When confronted, our students have no time for debate, only action, if they are to survive.

"Life is an opportunity, benefit from it. Life is a beauty, admire it. Life is a dream, realize it. Life is a challenge, meet it. Life is a duty, complete it. Life is a game, play it. Life is a promise, fulfill it. Life is sorrow, overcome it. Life is a song, sing it. Life is a struggle, accept it. Life is a tragedy, confront it. Life is an adventure, dare it. Life is luck, make it. Life is life, fight for it!"

~Mother Teresa

"Carved on these walls is the story of America, of a continuing quest to preserve both democracy and decency, and to protect a national treasure that we call the American dream."
~President George H.W. Bush

www.nleomf.com
www.nationalcops.org

Police Instructor

Table of Contents

"It's a funny thing about life; if you refuse to accept anything but the best, you very often get it."
~W. Somerset Maugham

SPIM

Super Police Instructor Man

Twilight hair so the girls dig him!

Super cool Ray-Ban sunglasses since he's Super Cool!

Gloves because John Wayne wore gloves!

Big biceps for the Gun Show!

Police logo t-shirt so everyone knows he's a Super Cool Cop!

A cape so cadets know to worship him!

Tall boots to wade through the crap from his stories!

SPIM is based on Officer Neil's real life s~~tory~~. EGO!

SPIM will keep you entertained with one of his factoids at the end of each chapter, and show you what it takes to be a Super Police Instructor!

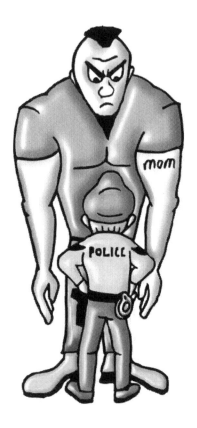

How Police Instructors are Made

I called out, *"Hold up a minute partner,"* as I patted him on the back. I was wondering if the guy was deaf. Just then, he swung around with a big haymaker. The punch glanced off the side of my head knocking me off balance. It didn't sink in right away that I was in for a nasty fight. It did not make any sense; I was just trying to be a nice guy and offer the man a ride home. Then his second punch hit me in the chest and my instincts decided they did not care if it made sense – *Just fight!*

We exchanged several more blows as I moved in close and grabbed his arm to no avail. Nature was obviously on his side as I only stood 5'9" tall (okay, 5'8½" but I like rounding up) and weighed in at 170 pounds. The monster I just provoked was 6'6" tall and weighed 260 pounds. I could sense it was not going to go well if we continued trading punches, so I swept his feet and took him to the ground. Luckily, he was not hurt by the big fall since he landed on top of me. He seemed surprised by my tenacity, but it was still obvious that he wanted a different outcome than I did. He was focused on kicking my butt and getting away while I was busy thinking that *this stuff doesn't happen here.*

I thought to myself, *I'm trained in defensive tactics; he should fear me.* BAM, he hit me in the face. *How rude! I can't believe this guy is assaulting a cop, that's against the law!* BAM, he hit me again. I thought about my extensive training in Army light infantry skills and then BAM, the guy hit me again! He did not seem to care about my résumé.

Once he knocked enough sense into me, I finally started to use my skills instead of just thinking about them. I landed several palm strikes that appeared to be devastating by the amount of blood they produced. He replied by punching my ear and educating me on the term *"wrung my bell."* I found myself on my back failing to fight off his attack. I knew I had no other option; I was going to have to kill him. I pulled my gun and prepared to fire, but then came a thud and blood sprayed over my face. *Did he hit me so hard that all I can see now is blood?* I pushed the gun into his side and began to pull the trigger, but before I could, he went limp and fell to the sidewalk.

> I pulled my gun and prepared to fire, but then came a thud and blood sprayed over my face.

Divine intervention had saved me from myself. There stood a frail old man with a big Maglite. He hit my attacker in the forehead knocking him for a loop. *"Thank you sir,"* was the first thing I had uttered since the beginning. That's right; I had not said a thing during the entire fight – no command to *"stop resisting!"* or otherwise. *"You saved me sir,"* I muttered as I handcuffed my first arrest. As I turned to ask him where he came from, he was gone. I never saw him again. Was it God who had saved me because He knew all the laughs I would bring Him throughout my career in law enforcement? That is an answer I will not get on this side of Heaven.

Did I fail my instructors, or did they fail me? Or, was it a little bit of both? I was second in my class academically and had the highest score on the state's written test the year I graduated, but neither seemed to matter on the street. I had only been out of the academy a few short weeks and had already ignored much of what was presented in class.

I had three days of field training before I was sent out on my own to protect a town with a population of 1800. It was my second weekend alone on patrol when I spotted the guy stumbling along. It was a cold February night, and I was sure he would appreciate my offer to drive him home. As I pulled over to the side of the road, I decided not to notify dispatch about the contact; it was just a friendly ride after all. This was only the first of many mistakes I made that night. When I yelled out *"How about a ride?"* he ignored me and kept on walking. Something did not feel right, but I ignored my intuition to call for backup and continued to approach him. I was too close when I reached out to pat him on his back which provided him the opportunity to hit me.

I did not give any commands and completely stopped breathing at times during the fight. I used my gun hand to pat him on the back and moved in without hesitation or thought. I did not consider pushing away at the first sign of hostility and going for pepper spray or using the opportunity to call for assistance. I allowed my thoughts of working in a small farm town betray me into thinking that nothing bad happens in such a place, and no one else had any idea what was happening on the sidewalk that night since I never called out. There are several good lessons that can be learned from this encounter that lasted just a few minutes – not only for students but instructors as well. Why did I fail to retain the lessons from my academy training?

The instructors failed to train me, and I failed to actively learn. The training should have prepared me for the real world of law enforcement, but I was shown little of value outside of what

> I allowed my thoughts of working in a small farm town to betray me into thinking that nothing bad happens in such a place.

was required to pass the test. And, there was no written test for me to take on that night.

The majority of my instructors opened the curriculum binder and began to read out loud starting us down the long boring road to wishing we were anywhere but in the police academy. On a rare occasion, we would have a truly advanced instructor who pulled out a piece of acetate and laid it on top of an overhead projector. Writing on a clear sheet of film with a black marker was about as progressive as we could hope for. That was to be repeated day after day for the better part of six months.

If you were like me, you caught yourself constantly drifting off wondering what police work was really like. Why were they keeping the truth from us? Did you long for the instructors that would provide a story or video showing exactly what the curriculum was trying to convey?

The few war stories that we heard had no relevance to the topic at hand, and they were told by instructors that wanted to be idolized by the cadets as a god among mere mortals. These instructors forgot their duty along the way – to serve the cadets as a trainer, role model, and inspirational guide into the world of law enforcement. When taken lightly, that duty can have devastating effects on the cadet and society. Today, we are doing better than our predecessors, but we can still do more.

Police Instructor – A Return to Prominence

Imagine you are a teenager visiting the local police department to write a story about becoming a law enforcement officer. You need to get different view points for your assignment so you talk to several officers. You approach the first officer in his patrol car ready to hit the street. You ask, *"What are you doing?"* He says, *"I'm making $20 an hour"* and drives away. For him, this is only a job. Hoping for more information, you find another officer who is placing her gear into a patrol car. You ask her, *"What are you doing?"* She gives a cynical answer, *"I'm writing reports and hanging out with dirt bags all day."* For her, law enforcement has become a burden. Still wanting something more for your story, you talk to an officer sitting at a desk. Filling out paperwork was not the example you wanted to write about, but you ask him anyway, *"What are you doing?"* The officer stops, turns to you with a smile, and explains, *"I am serving our community as a guardian of justice. I am fulfilling my oath to God, to protect and serve his people. Without my sacrifice there can be no justice. There can be no society."*

The officers share the same profession, but each has a different vision of law enforcement. Which vision do you inspire as an instructor? We need trainers who will passionately serve to build the guardians of tomorrow and to help them understand the importance of their commitment. Without sacrifice there can be no justice – there can be no society.

> Without sacrifice there can be no justice – there can be no society.

The recipe for a good police instructor includes generous portions of courage, patience, and stubbornness mixed with as much wisdom and humility as you can find. These traits, along with a determination to improve our craft, will provide skilled and worthy protectors for our society.

The Bible speaks of God, the *Potter* of all life, taking a lump of ordinary clay and forming it into a glorious work of art – unique from any other. Picture yourself as a potter with a lump of clay on your wheel (it shouldn't be hard to picture some of your students this way). As an instructor, you become part of the process of forming the clay into a unique person. You must take a cadet with *little* or *no* knowledge of law enforcement, and form them into a *guardian* of justice.

It will take time and energy to form the clay into such a person and you will probably get messy during the process, but it is well worth the effort. The FTO may put the final glazing on the guardian, but the work is started on the potter's wheel by the police instructor.

SPIM Factoid

SPIM is so strong that he created fire by rubbing two criminals together.

My Notes Ideas Cases Stories

Understanding Cops and Cadets

I was assigned as a school resource officer at one of the largest high schools in Ohio with 3,000 students and staff. My duties included investigating criminal activity, teaching in the classrooms, and protecting the school from predators and would-be attackers. It was not a program where I was just there to play nice and be their friend. I would be making arrests, investigating criminal conduct by students and teachers, and carrying a gun in their school, so making friends would not be an easy task. I decided to start by giving a presentation to every student in the school. The principal said I could write a letter and he would make the students read it (that paper would have been good for nothing but starting fires), but after some negotiating he agreed to interrupt the class schedule and give me time to present the SRO program. I delivered a dozen presentations over the following week.

The first day I had only one presentation scheduled. The 30 minute talk went well, but I had a few hecklers when I asked for questions. They wanted to know if I had bullets in my gun and if they could hold it. They were just teenage boys acting goofy in front of their friends, but I saw it as my opportunity to show them I had a personality and a sense of humor. I made some changes for the next day that I knew would be a hit if I were presenting to a group of cops, but I was not.

I employed a toy gun once used by a suspect to commit a robbery. It may have been a piece of plastic but it looked just like my Glock, and would serve my purpose well. I put it in the lectern and waited for the perfect moment to use the prop. The first two presentations were in the morning and went off with no cocky comments (they were all still sleeping or hung over). Finally I had a student ask the question I had been waiting for *"Can I hold your gun?" "You sure can,"* I replied.

I walked toward the teen with the toy Glock in my hand. He looked surprised when I said, *"You guys can just pass it around."* Then I acted as if I tripped and dropped it right in his lap. The entire assembly gasped as the boy jumped straight out of his seat squealing like my mother when she runs into a mouse. The toy hit the floor and I started laughing, *"It's just a toy, and No, you cannot hold my gun."* The assembly erupted in laughter, including the cocky boy who asked the stupid question. I was thinking *"I am the coolest cop ever!"* Then I saw the faces of the teachers and the principal in attendance, and it was obvious that they did not think it was cool at all.

I had not shared my gag with them, and they did not think it was funny. It seems educators do not necessarily share the same sense of humor as law enforcement and would be considered a different audience from our own. I apologized to those present and let the remaining staff members know that a toy gun would be involved in my presentation. It was a great method to break the ice with the students, but I did not consider my entire audience. I learned from my initial screw up but a few of the staff members never talked to me again – ever!

Knowing Your Audience

We have a specific type of audience with law enforcers and cadets, and valuable research is available to help us understand the best methods to use when instructing them. While there are always exceptions, most cops fit into a narrow set of general characteristics and traits. Cadets, on the other hand, have slightly greater diversity as a group and are commonly fun to teach. Cadets want to be in your class to learn from you while some veteran officers do not. In this chapter, you will gain insight that will help you develop more effective slide design and presentation techniques for these groups.

> We have a specific type of audience with law enforcers and cadets...

Since this chapter is based mostly on research, I will keep it brief and to the point. I want to start with some research on officer decertification. We will start with the bad and move through the good.

"Education without values, as useful as it is, seems rather to make man a more clever devil." ~C. S. Lewis

Understanding Why LEOs Get Into Trouble

One study from the Peace Officer Standards and Training Commissions and Councils provided valuable insight into the reasons why officers across the nation lose their certification.

The research found of the 3,884 cases the LEOs were employed as follows: 56% were city officers, although they comprise 66% of the workforce. 33% were county deputies, although they comprise 25% of the workforce. 11% were state officers, although they comprise 8% of the workforce.

The top 10 crimes for which officers were decertified included:
* False Statements/Reports 19.92%
* Larceny 12.12%
* Sex Offenses Other Than Rape 9.48%

* Battery 9.15%
* Driving Under The Influence 5.08%
* Excessive Use of Force 5.05%
* Fraud/Forgery 5.03%
* Drugs Other Than Cannabis/Cocaine 4.64%
* Weapon Offenses 4.02%
* Cocaine-Possession or Sell 3.08%

Other than filing false statements and reports, virtually all other offenses committed by the officers can be placed into four groups.

> Other than false statements & reports, virtually all other offenses committed by the officers can be placed into four groups.

Greed (26.99%)
* Larceny (12.12%)
* Fraud/Forgery (5.03%)
* Sell of Cocaine (3.08%)
* Sell of Cannabis (1.36%)
* Robbery (1.19%)
* Bribery (1.19%)
* Stolen Property (1.10%)
* Gambling (.46%)

Anger (19.69%)
* Battery (9.15%)
* Excessive Use of Force (5.05%)
* Weapon Offense (4.02%)
* Family Offense (1.47%)

Lust (12.74%)
* Sexual Offenses Other Than Rape (9.48%)
* Sexual Battery/Rape (2.77%)
* Morals-Decency Crimes (.49%)

Peer Pressure (12.70%)
* Driving Under The Influence (5.08%)
* Drugs Other Than Cocaine & Cannabis (4.64%)
* Cocaine (1.62%)
* Cannabis (1.36%)

One surprising finding was the average age for decertification – 32 years. With the focus of ethics training at the academy level, we can miss the reality that many of these officers were veteran law enforcers. The average time in service when the decertification process had begun was 7.2 years. Officers with 5–10 years of service, and not rookies, are those most likely to act unethically. Ethics should not be taught as a one-time class during the police academy, but as a critical component of every topic taught throughout an officer's career.

The officers in the study are the exception in a profession filled with the finest America has to offer. Our noble profession consistently draws people who are duty bound and feel the calling to serve others with integrity and courage. Take the time and determine where ethics can fit into your presentation, and keep our standards high.

Ingredients of a Cop

It is important for us to see each person as an individual – not just as part of a group – to connect with them and engage them as learners. A study in the *Journal of Police and Criminal Psychology* (Hogan and Kurtines, *2005)* found that experienced police officers were different from the general public in several ways:

- ☆ They were more assertive
- ☆ They showed more potential for social mobility
- ☆ They had more social poise and self confidence
- ☆ They had a more pronounced sense of self worth
- ☆ They had more need for independent achievement
- ☆ They had more functional intelligence
- ☆ They had more psychological-mindedness
- ☆ They were more masculine
- ☆ They possessed greater empathy

This one study lets us know that cops are confident in their abilities and have the skills to communicate with just about anyone. They are clever; they have street smarts and common sense. And of course they (we) have a bit of an ego, and enjoy competition and individual recognition.

A study of cadets from three different academies (Hargrave and Hiatt 1989) found that better adjusted cadets performed better in training. The successful cadets displayed better functional intelligence and were more outgoing and sociable individuals. Recruits were described as extroverts who were venturesome and impulsive. Cadets are a mini-me of the average law enforcer but are usually more open minded.

Three Basic Learning Types

There are three major types of learners: visual, auditory, and kinesthetic. They are sometimes referred to as the Fleming's VARK model. There are other models, but Fleming's is widely used and easy to understand and apply. Everyone has a unique way of learning:

* Visual learners like pictures, handouts, and slide shows involving videos.
* Auditory learners want to hear your presentation and function well with lectures and class discussions. They learn best by reading out loud to fully understand written material.
* Kinesthetic learners like to experience the topic through touch. Firearms, driving, and other physical skills are where these learners feel at home. If you just lecture a kinesthetic group, they will be squirming in their chairs.

Our audience consists mostly of kinesthetic and visual learners, but they have an auditory need as well. We should strive to add a visual and kinesthetic component to all of our lectures and give students an opportunity to put their hands and eyes on the material.

"American teachers have one indisputable advantage...they understand the American temperament and can judge its unevenness, its lights and its shadows." ~John Philip Sousa

Extroverted vs. Introverted

60% of all learners are extroverts and the vast majority of all cops and cadets are as well. We seldom have an introverted person in an academy class that sits passively by and fears interaction. You have to be outgoing and sociable to function well in law enforcement and introverts rarely want in.

Extroverted learners like spending their time around other people and generating ideas as a group. They learn best by teaching others and solving problems. They like to lead during group assignments and normally jump right in without much coaching on your part.

Most cadets tend to be realistic and practical, preferring to rely on information gained through experience. While cadets work well with order and routine, they also tend to be very quick to adapt to changing environments and situations. They will focus on the present, and they use common sense to solve problems while constantly observing the world around them. They want reality in the classroom and enjoy case studies describing their future duties as law enforcers.

These are not the type of students who look forward to slide shows full of bullet points and long boring lectures. If you enjoy being an instructor, learning by experience, and are not afraid to work in a group, you are an extroverted learner yourself. Make learning interactive and you will have their undivided attention.

"There are some things you learn best in calm, and some in storm". ~Willa Cather

The Type A's

We are accused of being *Type A* personalities all the time in law enforcement, and it is usually true (it is for me). The personality types were originally developed to determine your likelihood of heart disease – not to use for educational purposes, but we gain insight knowing that cops generally have more *Type A* traits.

The *A* individual is described as ambitious, aggressive, business-like, controlling, highly competitive, impatient, preoccupied with status, time-conscious, and tightly-wound (sounds like qualifications for a politician). *A's* are commonly diagnosed with free-floating hostility or aggressiveness which is seen as impatience, rudeness, and having a short fuse (sounds like morning roll call). Their behavior also includes a strong orientation towards achievement, and *A's* usually have demanding and stressful professions (like cops). They are also known to become socially isolated within their professional group.

The *Type B* personalities are generally patient, relaxed, easy-going, and at times lacking any sense of urgency. You will have cadets who fall clearly under *B*, but they are in the minority. This is the new rookie that gets fired for being late to work three days in a row. Nothing is an urgent need to them – not even policing.

There is also a *Type AB* personality for people who cannot be clearly categorized as either *A* or *B*. Many of our cops and cadets share traits from both *types*.

This information has been around since the 1950's, and it makes me wonder why so much training in the law enforcement world is lecture-based. *What in the Type A traits says "lecture me?"*

Teaching Social Cyborgs

Army warriors now receive advanced training using social networks, online games, and information technology. The military training courses using social learning technologies showed a 30% increase in student achievement and a 30% reduction in training time and costs. Following their initial review, the Defense Department recommended that all its training begin implementing network-based education wherever appropriate. It should by no means become the only form of training, but it has obvious value for our warriors as well.

> Social learning technologies showed a 30% increase in student achievement...

Like it or not, we must begin to evolve our training methods and strategies for today's learners. We can start by understanding what some have deemed as a generation of *Social Cyborgs*. A Cyborg is a science fiction creation in which a human takes on super powers through some mechanical enhancement, but if you would have told me 25 years ago that I would hold a computer in the palm of my hand that connects me directly with billions of users, I would have said that was science fiction as well.

Social Cyborg describes the people who have integrated social networks and the information highway into the way they think, learn, and solve problems. We are training recruits that have never known a world without the Internet, smart phones, online gaming, or MP3 players. They are in constant contact with others just like them, and they take full advantage of the vast network of information and people available – so should we.

As part of Generation X, I watched as technology developed, but it was never a significant factor in my education, Army training, or early policing career. I grew to love some technologies and hate others. I still struggle with some today, but the *millennial* generation embraces them as part of their *being*. If they need to research a problem for school or learn a new skill to work on the kitchen sink, they can find a YouTube tutorial, Wiki information resource, or social network of experts.

We do not have to start by creating the newest butt-kicking video game to engage our learners (though it would be used more often than the Revised Code websites). We can begin by incorporating network-based learning through *LEO* centered blogs or forums like those at Linkedin.com, LawOfficer.com, PoliceOne.com, and others. They can provide recruits with new locations to network and new methods to find relevant law enforcement information from across the globe. Challenging activities and problem solving tasks that promote group learning are a great way to reach the *Social Cyborgs* in your class.

> We are training recruits that have never known a world without the Internet, smart phones, online gaming, or MP3 players.

Making it Work for Everyone

Pulling all this information together can be done with a little effort. If you concentrate on the three types of learners and use the rest of the information to guide your interactions with students, the class will be a success. Remember most of your cadets will learn effectively using all three learning styles – they will just favor one over the others. Here are a few simple examples of how to use the information with a class of cadets:

Topic: Juvenile Justice

Show a short video clip from the documentary *Murder on Sunday Morning* of a 15 year old arrested in Jacksonville, Florida in 1996 for a murder he did not commit. He was later acquitted and the right person arrested. This will appeal to your auditory audience as well as your visual learners.

Have cadets debate whether the officers' actions in falsely arresting the innocent juvenile were criminal or just unethical. Have them write down and present their decisions to the class. The debate will appeal to all three learning styles, but especially the kinesthetic learners.

Topic: *Crime Scene Investigation*

Show photographs of a homicide scene during your slide show. The visual learners will definitely be engaged through investigative images. Tell the story of the case and explain step by step how it was solved. The story will pull in the auditory learners. Have the students practice the fingerprinting method used to identify the suspect. Now the kinesthetic learners are also fully engaged with your lesson. Include a talk on the *Exclusionary Rule* to add an *ethics* component to the topic, and you have a well rounded class.

Topic: *Missing Persons*

Hand out maps covering your local area. Give students a scenario of a lost Alzheimer's patient and let them plot out their search areas as a team. Have them write down assignments and make an action plan to find the person as quickly as possible. Have each team explain their plan of action to the class, and then compare the different approaches used by the groups. All three types of learners will be engaged throughout the exercise.

Why do we need to mix it up so much? Cadets and cops need to think on their feet. Law enforcement is not a profession where you can always intellectualize your way out of a situation. If someone is punching you in the face, it's best not to get caught up on why – just do something about it.

It should not be our mission to create great test takers. Our mission must be to make effective guardians for society. Memorizing every SPO (Student Performance Objective is Ohio's training term) will not make a person into a great cop, or keep them alive. Only one part of their training should be dedicated to tests and academic work. The other part has to demand students to perform at a higher level of understanding in *every* topic by engaging all of their senses in the learning process.

"Know your stuff. Know whom you are stuffing. Know when they are stuffed." ~Anonymous

More than a Transfer of Information

If you are a police instructor, I can assume you have experience, knowledge, skill, commitment, integrity, passion, and vision. Use these traits and characteristics to design presentations that are easy to follow and understand. Remember to focus the presentation on your audience and they will focus on you.

Our mission is not to simply transfer information to our audience – but to help them change in some measurable way. If information transfer is all you want to accomplish, give them a handout and let them go home early. As a police instructor, you have the duty to inspire your audience to learn something of value from you – not your handouts or your slide show. You provide the wisdom that might one day save their life. They need to learn new skills that they do not have, and they will not, unless you are engaging and passionate about training them. How you come across *personally* with law enforcers may be more important than everything else combined.

> How you come across *personally* with law enforcers may be more important than everything else combined.

SPIM Factoid
Prison graveyards have signs that say "SPIM was here."

Planning and Preparation Shortcuts

The cars were lined up ready to travel across the new bridge. Their small town would finally be united with the city across the river. It would save the citizens 45 minutes of driving to get to the stores, the schools, and the only hospital. The people raised millions of dollars and donated hundreds of hours to make the project work. The mayor cut the ribbon, but before the first car could cross, the engineer made an announcement. He told the people, "I did not use design plans, follow construction requirements, or perform any safety tests on the structure. However, I assure you that it is safe to cross."

The citizens were shocked and appalled. They refused to drive across the bridge with their families at risk. *How could he be so reckless?*

The engineer was insulted – he was an expert after all. He knew what he was doing. *What more did they want?*

Would you cross the bridge with your kids in the car? Would you be upset after investing time and money in the project? Walking into a presentation with nothing more than your expertise in law enforcement is the same as building a bridge without plans. It is a disaster waiting to happen. Students invest hundreds of hours and thousands of dollars to attend your academy, and they should see a presentation with design plans – not an instructor who decided to *wing it.*

A poorly constructed bridge appears to be more dangerous than a poorly trained police officer – but the bridge will only collapse once. The law enforcer may be around for decades impacting the lives of thousands of citizens and endangering his fellow officers.

It is a noble endeavor to serve as a police instructor, but you must develop essential qualities to succeed. You need determination over discouragement, enthusiasm to train law enforcers, and the self-confidence to believe you will succeed.

> You need determination over discouragement, enthusiasm to train law enforcers, and the self-confidence to believe you will succeed.

"Education will not take the place of persistence; the world is full of educated derelicts. Persistence and determination alone are omnipotent. The slogan 'press on' has solved and always will solve the problems of the human race." ~Calvin Coolidge

LEO Engineer

As an instructor, you are the engineer of your presentation. Your expertise is the greatest value the cadets can receive, but without planning and preparation they will be confused much of the time. You may know what you mean during your talk but they will not. It is all new to them.

Do not use the old excuses: *"I'm better off the cuff,"* or *"I don't want to sound rehearsed,"* or the most common *"I don't have time to prepare anything; I'm too busy."* This is what I refer to as crap, double crab, and lazy crap. It is all crap! If you want to *wing it* with a 3 minute speech, have at it, but when you are teaching cops and cadets, you owe it to society to invest some time and effort to make it significant. If you give any less, you are building a bridge without plans, without meeting construction requirements, and without any testing. Structurally, it will be doomed.

> This is what I refer to as crap, double crab, and lazy crap.

Many of us don't look forward to the preparation of a presentation and even fewer want to practice before the actual delivery, but it is a necessary step to make citizens into cadets and cadets into guardians.

Research Your Topic

Even if you have a curriculum provided to you, it is always best to do some research. Once a curriculum is written it quickly becomes dated, but you can make it fresh by adding new information. It is easy to find relevant and current stories on police websites – no profession is covered quite like ours. When you add a recent story to the topic, it shows the class that you prepared the presentation personally. They will recognize you as an instructor who takes the time and makes the effort to personalize your material. By adding your own handouts, group activities, and stories, you make it your own.

Collect more material than you will use. It is better to have too much than not enough when you first start building your presentation or slide show. With a vast quantity of information you can find the great stuff and throw out the rest, but keep the quirky and unusual points that others might not think to use. That is what *grabs* an audience. Through diligent research and unique ideas you will prove that you consider their time valuable.

Sticky Notes Layout

At some point, you will have to stop researching and start preparing. Decide how you want to organize your collection of material, and start putting it together into a presentation or slide show. Start out with a broad overview including several main points. Then develop sub-points and details that support your key message.

One method I like to use involves Post-It notes. Write each idea, item of information, or SPO on a separate note. Lay them out on the table or stick them to a wall. Picture them like slides in a *PowerPoint* presentation, and then move them around to see what order makes the most sense to you. You do not need every little detail on the notes. Instead, write just enough information to remind yourself of what will go on the actual slide. This method makes it easier to visualize your presentation than starting with the *PowerPoint* program first.

Some of us are easily distracted by using a computer with an Internet connection. We start our slide design, then log into our e-mail, check what movies are playing, and see what the weather will be tomorrow – one interruption after another. Sometimes, it can be more productive to get away from the online interruptions and go back to paper and pencil. Sticky notes are a great method for getting away from distractions, and you can take them wherever you feel like working.

Flexibility

There will be times when you end up with too much information in your presentation. Regardless of how much sweat you put into your slide show, you need to be flexible enough to skip some of your presentation if necessary. You should look strategically at the slides before hand, and then decide what you can leave out if you need too. When you are a dynamic speaker, you focus your presentation on the audience. That means you cannot always stick to an exact plan or pace. A discussion that goes long may prove to be beneficial, but it will require a change in your agenda. Do what is best for your audience and help them gain the knowledge from your topic that will most benefit them.

Use a Theme

There are books and workshops dedicated to the development of *themes* for stories and presentations. Regardless of your topic, themes are an effective principle to enhance your presentations for an academy or in-service training, and it will help the learner retain the information by keeping everything connected. Be creative when considering your theme; even a quote can motivate your audience.

"Life is either a daring adventure, or nothing." ~Helen Keller

You must choose several sub-points that will trace back to the theme as your presentation moves along. A theme provides a flow for your audience, and it increases their attentiveness as they watch for the next piece of the puzzle. This process not only works well with our law enforcement topics but adds intrigue and curiosity instead of boredom. The following is an example of how you can develop a theme with a current curriculum you are assigned to teach.

Our instructors complain about the *Foot Patrol* topic as a short and boring block to teach – if left unenhanced – they are correct. I have chosen it here to prove a point that we can use different techniques to make any curriculum interesting and beneficial for our audience.

Topic: Foot Patrol 8-2

The objectives for the topic include *SPO#1 - The 9 Advantages of Foot Patrol* and *SPO#2 - The 7 Disadvantages of Foot Patrol.* Nothing about that jumps out at a cadet and says, *"This will be cool to learn."* By adding a theme, you add interest. Use the theme *"Surviving Foot Patrol"* on your opening slide along with an image of a dark alley. Now it sounds and looks like something that might be important for them to know.

As they settle in for class, the introductory slide will already be creating interest and concern in their minds. They will envision themselves holding a flashlight walking down a dark alley on the midnight shift. Under the theme of *"Surviving Foot Patrol,"* your sub-points should include the two SPOs, and two additional subjects not in the curriculum: *"Awareness Skills"* and *"Dangerous Encounters."*

Start with two quick questions of the class, *"When is foot patrol useful?"* and *"When is it dangerous?"* Many cadets will not connect danger or excitement to foot patrol because it does not sound scary or interesting. They think of *Officer Friendly* walking down the sidewalk speaking to citizens, and that is what they will continue to think if you allow it. This is where we can fail cadets in the academy. If we neglect to share our knowledge of the risks involved with foot patrol, and personal experiences with dangerous individuals, we leave our students unprepared. A cadet will have no real understanding of what it is like to walk into a dark alley unless you tell them about it.

After discussing the opening questions, cover the required SPOs as sub-points. Share the knowledge in each SPO as a benefit that will help them in *"Surviving Foot Patrol."* It connects the SPOs to your theme and makes an otherwise boring topic engaging and relevant. Move to your third sub-point of *"Awareness Skills"* and cover the signs of danger. Show students several short videos of suspects making furtive movements. Challenge them to look for *red flags* in body language and signs of concealed weapons. Show pictures of the tools to look for on a suspected burglar – screwdrivers, crowbars, scanners, etc... Point back to your theme and show how the *"Awareness Skills"* just covered can save their life on the street.

Use the most persuasive and compelling sub-point, *"Dangerous Encounters,"* for a powerful finish. Use stories of officers who were injured or killed in the line of duty while on foot

> A cadet will have no real understanding of what it is like to walk into a dark alley unless you tell them about it.

patrol. On January 1, 2011 *Deputy Suzanne Hopper* was out *on foot* investigating a report of a window that had been shot out of a trailer. It was a Saturday morning and most residents in the trailer park were sleeping in from *New Years Eve* celebrations. She was about to take photographs of a shoe impression when the suspect opened the door to his trailer and shot and killed her without warning.

I knew *Deputy Hopper* and her story can be hard to tell, but that is how we pay tribute to those who have sacrificed everything in their role as a guardian of justice. Using a photo of a fallen officer along with our theme can inject reality into the classroom.

The short one hour block of foot patrol is now an effective and engaging part of the cadets' training, and it should be, since we know they will spend plenty of time *on foot* in this profession. Always point back to the main theme throughout your presentation, and they will recall your nuggets of wisdom forever. We should never take it for granted that a well-instructed one hour block on *Foot Patrol* could very well save a life.

> We should never take it for granted that a well-instructed one hour block on *Foot Patrol* could very well save a life.

"Wisdom is knowing what to do next; skill is knowing how to do it, and virtue is doing it." ~David Starr Jordan

Never Try to Memorize Your Material

Memorization is a trap that destroys effectiveness for instructors who do not trust in their knowledge and experience. Focus on your ideas and not on words. A few notes on the lectern, or hints in a slide show, should be enough to remind you of your message and its key points. Memorization sounds mechanical and it is unnecessary.

We speak with others spontaneously. We think in ideas – if our ideas are clear, the words will come without memorization.

When you have a script or read from a curriculum, it will always sound monotone to your audience; you are speaking from memory and not from the heart. When you talk to your friends and family, you don't rehearse. Instead, you base your conversation on your knowledge, experience, and beliefs. The same method is what you should use when you train guardians.

"Written things are not for speech; their form is literary; they are still, inflexible, and will not lend themselves to happy effective delivery with the tongue... they have to be limbered up, broken up, colloquialized, and turned into the common form of unpremeditated talk; otherwise they will bore the house – not entertain it." ~Mark Twain

Always Review Out Loud

Read your presentation out loud and make sure it sounds as good as it looks. By reading it out loud, you will know what it sounds like for your students, and how long it will take. We read silently at a different pace than we speak. Time it, and you will see the difference. If something does not sound right to you, it definitely will not sound right to them – fix it.

Put yourself in the students place to make sure there is a flow throughout your presentation that they can follow. Will they understand it as well as you? Continue to tighten and reshape your raw information until you have a final dynamic delivery.

Practice Makes ~~Perfect~~ Permanent

Like it or not, you need to prepare and then practice your presentation. That alone eliminates most of the undue stress we experience before teaching. When you know the material well, you do not have to worry about it during your presentation. You can never know it well enough to be perfect, and trying to do so is counterproductive. Just get familiar with what you have created, and you will be well on your way.

Rehearse with Friends and Family

You do not have to wait until you have your presentation completed to start practicing your delivery. Once you develop a key point and have some idea of what you want to teach your students, try it out on your family and friends. This method is easier than standing in front of a mirror and talking with yourself (and less embarrassing).

Do not let your friends and family know you are trying to sneak in a practice session at their expense. Begin to use the ideas you have developed for your presentation in everyday conversations. When you bring up the information, watch how they respond to your explanation and viewpoint. They may provide you with great feedback and unexpected questions.

If you are able to keep the practice a mystery with your friends, you successfully instructed using a natural delivery. The same method should be used when you are standing in front of your class. It may help you uncover points of contention that people have with your topic, as well as facts that you may have missed.

Do not wait until you have assembled a presentation for the 24 hour block on *Community Diversity* before starting to practice. It can be overwhelming to consider practicing the material for such a long topic, but it becomes easier if you are continually inserting the information into your daily conversations.

Trust Your Intuition

As you create your presentation and slide show, the process may generate thoughts and memories you did not anticipate. Some may be useful to the class you are teaching. Do not fight the inclination to add the new material as long as it is relevant to the topic. Creating a good presentation does not necessarily mean you must follow a specific blueprint or structure. Everyone is different, and only you can figure out what works best for you.

You should not be upset when your first layout does not feel quite right. Any new program will lack clarity and have some stuff that needs to be fixed. Initially, it may sound boring and need fine-tuning, but trust your intuition and it will come together.

The best instructors are constantly fiddling with their format, slides, handouts, and materials to make the entire presentation better. Learn to

> Creating a good presentation does not necessarily mean you must follow a specific blueprint or structure.

enjoy the fiddling, and the feeling that comes from knowing your next audience is in for an encounter – not just an education.

"There is creative vision in each of us, but sometimes it's hard to get that creative part started."
~Barbara Januszkiewicz

You Can't Force Feed Wisdom

Never measure your success by how much information you can force on your class in a short amount of time. Instead, base it on how well they understood the information you presented. *Did you provide them with something of value that will benefit them as a law enforcement officer? Can they actually perform the skills you demonstrated, or did they just memorize another SPO?*

If you are an expert on *Arson*, you will not be able to shove all of your experience into the one hour block allotted by the state for *Arson Investigation*. In such a format, your duty is not to create arson investigators but to familiarize cadets with the evidence and perpetrators associated with such crimes. The information should be relevant and concise, and just enough to be absorbed in the amount of time provided.

When you find yourself with a limited amount of time, try not to speed through the information. If you have more information than time, consider providing it to your students in a handout instead of rushing through a slide show. The presentation will not be as effective if you rush through the material. Decide what *must* be kept, and what you can *remove*. Challenge your students to research the topic further by providing them with websites, books, or cases to study. Create an interest for them that will benefit them throughout their career.

My Topic Sucks!

When you are assigned a topic that sucks, it is a good idea to ask yourself a couple of questions, *"What can go right if I do a good job?"* and *"What can go wrong if I do not?"*

We all have subject areas that we do not particularly like to instruct. I find myself complaining each time I am assigned a topic I do not like to teach, but it still needs to be taught – and taught well. Consider starting off with a topic you do not want to teach. It forces you to step out of your comfort zone and find something unique to make the topic persuasive – not only so your students will learn, but also so you will enjoy teaching it.

Whether it is through humor, stories, or videos, you can captivate an audience long enough to ensure they take away knowledge from your class. Look for a new perspective on the subject, and you may find more value in the topic than was on the surface. Show the audience that you have put energy into making the topic more engaging, and they will want to explore the results of your efforts. If you say *"This is just a boring topic,"* you have already failed them as an instructor. The personal experience you share with your audience should be enough inspiration to ensure the presentation is not boring regardless of the underwhelming subject.

If you believe your talents and expertise are being wasted on a boring topic, it will show to the class. It will appear as though you have put yourself on a pedestal believing you are too good for such a lowly topic. It breaks the connection we have with our audience when we waste their time by not putting any effort into the presentation. After all, it is our duty to provide students with knowledge – not complain about our assignment.

Running Long and Staying After

If you find yourself running out of time, make sure you give the class all the required information before they leave. Do not make students responsible for finding the material you should have provided them. The sight of an instructor rushing out of the classroom ahead of their students is embarrassing to watch.

Plan your time so you are available after class for questions, and if you cannot stay a few minutes after, consider finding a topic that demands less time from your schedule. Students have trouble believing the material is important if you did not prepare or stick around to answer questions. As instructors, we can model professionalism by always respecting our students' time – even if they do not respect ours.

Finishing Strong

A compelling ending for your presentation is just as important as the beginning. If you end by taking questions, you risk an *irrelevant* question and answer being the last thing students hear.

For whatever reason, we commonly leave our ending out of the planning and preparation process – I have made this mistake myself. We think something will just come to us at the end and we will wrap up just fine. I am not saying a street-smart cop cannot *wing it* with some cadets and get by. But I don't want to just get by, I want each student to have a lasting impression of my theme and leave a better person. Instead of *winging it,* plan the ending of your presentation to create a powerful connection that will last long after you have gone.

It does not reflect well on us as instructors to run out of material long before our time is up and then try to blame it on the curriculum. There are great activities in *Police Instructor* like *Quiz Five-0 Style* that you can use for an engaging review if you run short. Saying *"I hope there was something useful in there,"* or *"It's not my fault, it's just a boring topic,"* will not make you appear professional or help your students.

What message would you like students to remember about your presentation tomorrow, next week, or next year? That message is what your ending should be. Leave enough time to drive home your *theme* before ending your presentation, and let that be the lasting impression in the students' minds as they walk away.

Follow Lincoln's Example

When you mention Abraham Lincoln, people recall his *Gettysburg Address* or words from one of his inaugural speeches. The 16th president wrote his own speeches and did not use a team of speechwriters like today's politicians. He took the responsibility to write his letters and speeches and that gave him an ownership that most other presidents do not share.

President Lincoln was known to practice his speeches several times in front of different cabinet members before he delivered them. His original speeches show scratched out words and additions to the original text because he was always improving upon what he had.

Even while running a country that was on the brink of civil war, Abe Lincoln created his own speeches and then practiced each one before delivering it to his audience. He didn't rely on a cookie cutter speech from previous administrations.

The time and effort you put into our cops and cadets will benefit the whole of society. If President Lincoln could find the time to prepare, so can we.

Planning & Preparation Shortcuts

It is not hard to get a good presentation together but the motivation to actually practice it can be tough. I enjoy the process of starting with very little and creating a compelling encounter for my audience, but it takes more than that. I am in as much danger as every other instructor of underestimating the importance of practicing.

I have more time to prepare than those of you still working in law enforcement, but I have lost the daily interactions that kept policing fresh in my mind. Active law enforcers make some of the best instructors, but it is still important for them to invest the time and effort necessary for planning. The cadets we train will one day be standing watch over society, so do your part and build a bridge that will be strong enough to support them for generations to come.

Preparation may not be your favorite topic to read about or my favorite topic to write about, but this is where the good trainers become great ones. There really are no great short cuts – just tips and techniques that I can offer throughout this book. I used *Shortcuts* in the title to entice you to read the chapter. It may have been a sneaky ploy, but then again, *I'm a cop – not a saint.*

"We all want progress, but if you're on the wrong road, progress means doing an about-turn and walking back to the right road; in that case, the man who turns back soonest is the most progressive." ~C. S. Lewis

SPIM Factoid

SPIM arranges his M&M's in alphabetical order while blindfolded.

Confidence is Power

Mark Twain made more money speaking at events across America than he did from his writing. He was the most renowned speaker of his time and delivered hundreds, if not thousands, of speeches throughout his life. We are in good company when we find ourselves nervous before a presentation.

"There are two types of speakers. Those who get nervous, and those who are liars." ~Mark Twain

People speak in public every day – more so if you are a cop. You talk to victims, witnesses, and suspects, and you convince large groups of people to calm down after tense situations.

Public speaking is simply having a conversation with a group. Most cops have the gift of gab and enjoy talking to random people on the street. Those are the qualities that make a good cop a better investigator, and a great instructor.

People Fear Speaking More Than Death?

The most quoted myth in public speaking – *"People fear public speaking more than death"* – is hogwash (a technical term for *lie*). There are dozens of bestselling books and articles that continue citing the myth as truth. It is used by some as a tactic to scare off the competition and by others who want to sell you some secret to overcome it. Either way, it is dishonest when they know it is not true.

These so called *experts* provide footnotes for everything else in their publications, but you will not see any such reference for the *"People fear public speaking more than death"* myth. It took a smidgen of my investigative skill to find out the statement came from a 1977 book by David Wallechinsky called *The Book of Lists*. It is a trivia book that has no scientific research on public speaking or death. People were asked what came to mind as their greatest fears, but not if speaking in public scared them more than death itself.

> The most quoted myth in public speaking – *"People fear public speaking more than death"* – is hogwash...

Think about it with just a little logic. Picture a guy giving someone the following choice to make. *"Listen buddy, you have two options. I'm either going to blow your head off, or you can speak in public. Which is it going to be?"* What do you think the average person in that situation would say? *"Please just blow my head off sir. I am so afraid of talking in front of people that I would rather my family and friends go on without me."* Really, that is what most people would do? I don't think so either. It is silly that it was believed in the first place, but truly sad that it has been passed on as truth. What is the problem caused by the myth? People believe it. Like anything, if you hear something enough it becomes the accepted truth. By knowing that public speaking is not a natural fear, you can be more confident the next time you present.

> *"A lie can go halfway around the world before the truth even has its shoes on."* ~Mark Twain

Safety Increases for Police Instructors

I believe we are safer as police instructors than at any other time in our lives. Consider my non-scientific theory for one moment. If you are teaching an in-service class to a group of police officers, you are surrounded by people with guns and badges that are sworn to protect you – even if your presentation sucks. Who else has that many cops surrounding them as a virtual shield from harm? Most dignitaries do not have that many armed guards protecting them, and if you are teaching a class of unarmed cadets, you can order them to shield you with their bodies. They are usually too afraid to question your directions, and that should give you ample time to get to safety. You can probably use the story later as a teaching point on critical thinking.

If you have a heart attack at home, no one will notice and you might die! But as a police instructor (hopefully teaching a class on first aid), it will be obvious to the entire class that you are in need. Most of them will know CPR; some may be closet EMTs, and everyone will know exactly who to call for help. How much safer could you get? I have no actual research to support this theory, and I admit that their assistance in your time of need may be partially based on how good or bad your presentation was, but that is another good reason for you to be a dynamic presenter.

Getting Started

The more confidence you have in your material, the more power you get from it. To increase your confidence, you must first work on anxiety and nerves that emerge during your presentation and turn them into extra energy. You should expect a certain amount of stage fright, but that can be resolved easily – practice, practice, practice. Only a prepared instructor will be fully confident in their presentation, and the audience will notice.

I have watched as instructors fumbled through an impromptu presentation. These officers became helpless and baffled with their lack of preparation and practice, floundering and apologizing while trying to make sense out of a curriculum they had never looked at. You would not respond to an armed robbery without your weapon, body armor, or back-up. You prepare at the beginning of each shift to ensure you are ready for whatever the world throws at you. So why would you train guardians without taking the time to effectively prepare? If you are reading this book – you do not.

If you are nervous when you start, it is a good idea to practice your opening a little more than the rest. Most of us calm down once we get started, and by knowing the first five minutes *well*, it helps us get through the anxious beginning.

"With the possible exception of the equator, everything begins somewhere." ~C. S. Lewis

Some instructors shoot themselves in the foot from the very beginning (no pun intended for the agent who did). They start out weak with a monotone, boring, and irrelevant opening that highlights their personal exploits and lengthy bio. The audience will decide if we should be in the front of the room or not regardless of our bio or attempts to convince them of our greatness.

Start with something memorable, and choose a strong theme to draw your audience in right from the beginning. People remember the beginning and end more than any other parts of a presentation. Make both powerful.

There are speakers who say you have less than 5 minutes to make a lasting impression with your audience, and others who only give you 60 seconds. They are both right depending on the audience. With police cadets, you have more time to impress them since they are eager to learn and excited to have the opportunity to be there. Veteran cops on the other hand may not even give you 60 seconds. They may not want to be there in the first place but you can quickly earn their interest, and eventually their trust, if you start out with something powerful. By showing them the benefit of your presentation, you will gain their attention and interest.

You can start with a personal story, a unique fact, or a controversial quote. Just about any way to start out with a bang will work. Consider looking for a point of contention relevant to the topic, and exploit it to fuel a debate among your students. Dispute, even anger among them, shows interest in your topic. These emotions are a daily occurrence for law enforcers and they will benefit from this type of learning experience.

I will take debate and anger any day over boredom and sleeping, but some instructors cannot handle the thought, or feeling, of losing control. They would rather lecture without involving their students and maintain complete dominion over the class. There can be little gained by anyone in this type of learning environment.

> I will take debate and anger any day over boredom and sleeping...

How to Gain Respect

When you gain respect and credibility, you will rarely have a major issue with a disruptive student, and that will help to build your confidence. There are a few simple rules to follow with law enforcers.

* Be yourself. If you are a jerk and no one likes you, please do us all a favor and stop instructing.

* Give a *brief* introduction and let your presentation prove you are the right person to teach the topic. When you are busy providing the audience with knowledge and wisdom, you will be gaining their respect. It highlights your credibility when you do not waste their time.

* Share with them everything of value and cut out the fluff. Cops hate fluff, but that is what 50% of some law enforcement classes are (a few of the books as well). The nuggets of wisdom you have uncovered during your career should be shared first. Let students know that you are not holding back important information like so many of our brethren do when they teach. It is no great secret that some cops do not *share* well with others. They learn something new and refuse to share it so they can feel superior or

special. It is through sharing that our profession grows in character, and society becomes safer.

⭐ Tell students about your training, experience, and research with the topic. Make it clear that you are also constantly learning and do not have every answer. If you don't know, say you don't know – they will respect you for it. If you find the answer during a break and provide it when class resumes, they will respect you even more. It shows that you are there to serve them – not the other way around.

The audience wants proof that their time is not going to be wasted by listening to your message. It does not matter if you are teaching a conference workshop or a classroom of cadets, be passionate and knowledgeable about your topic. Audiences would rather listen to a nervous speaker who has real knowledge than an arrogant speaker who can only talk about the subject in theory.

Cops make Great Speakers

I have been to conferences with notable speakers that were entertaining but failed to provide the audience with anything of real value. They had degrees in communication, journalism, or public speaking, but lacked the life experiences that would benefit others. At one event, I saw a law enforcer follow the main speaker; he was far more engaging. He was having a conversation with his audience and provided them with the wisdom that comes from making critical decisions every day. He was passionate about his message and wanted to share his lesson with the audience.

While he did not have formal training or credentials qualifying him as a great speaker, he had confidence in his experience. His knowledge came from real life encounters, and reality is what interests people most. As a police instructor, you *must* be *eager* to share your message with the audience you serve. To be effective there is no getting around this principle. You *must* look deep into the topic and make it your personal *desire* to help each student *see* the value in your presentation.

Effective police instructors will find a *personal* connection with the topic and inject themselves into the presentation.

Nothing is more appealing to listeners than your personal experience with the subject. *Nothing!*

Be Honest

Honesty and integrity should be modeled for our students each time they see us. Richard Jr. was nine years old when he taught me what honesty was supposed to look like.

He caught a ground ball hit to him at second base. He tagged the runner who was advancing to second and threw the ball to first for a double play. The umpire yelled, *"You're out."* I was jumping up and down – my kid just turned a double play! Richard stepped forward and caught the umpire's attention by waiving his glove and yelling, *"He's safe, I missed him."* Everyone stopped and looked silently as he repeated, *"I missed him sir; he was safe."* The umpire ordered the player he had just called *out* back to second base. Richard's coach started to scorn him for his honesty. Even the other coach was shaking his head in response to the unprovoked confession.

I stepped out onto the field and told my son that he had just made me the proudest father in the ballpark. He had done what was right – not what was commonly practiced – but what was right. I scorned the coaches for their attitudes that encouraged the players to lie (having a gun and badge helped to get the point across). Somehow lying was acceptable while the players were on the field, but they expected the kids to stop when the game was over. Both coaches apologized to Richard and the umpire applauded him. His coach later insisted on his players telling the truth regardless of the outcome of a game, and sportsmanship was once again the focus of playing the sport.

We can easily adopt a belief that is not a true representation of *who* we are simply because it has become a norm. If something in your training needs changed, then change it. Regardless of the past practice of others, or the consequences, we should always model honesty and integrity. If it was easy to be a police instructor, every cop would do it.

Answer the Why

Inspire students by sharing relevant information, and they will learn each time they have you as an instructor. You want them to be satisfied with your presentation but not overwhelmed by the material you are presenting. If they still want to hear more from you, that is a good thing.

"Be who you are and say what you feel, because those who mind don't matter, and those who matter don't mind."
~Dr. Seuss

A good way to start is by telling them *why* you are a cop and *why* you instruct cadets. Not what you *do* as a cop, but *why* you do it. Sure, they may be interested to find out you are on the SWAT team or specialize in traffic reconstruction, but that does not engage them with your message. Cadets want to know *why* you do those things – a secret missed by many instructors – and a far more interesting way to start.

Before you finish a presentation, you should answer two questions for your audience: *"What was the point?"* and *"Why should it matter?"*

Eye Contact

Keep eye contact with your students just as you would in a one-to-one conversation. Do not picture people naked, or stare at a spot on the wall, or follow any other dumb advice. Make natural eye contact and the audience will connect with you.

Look at a student long enough that they notice your eye contact and then move on to someone else. With a large audience, make eye contact with different people spread throughout the crowd. With a small class, make eye contact with each person as you move through your presentation. The point of eye contact is to make the individual audience member feel noticed as if you were presenting everything directly to them.

"Make eye contact. Eye contact emphasizes sincerity and without sincerity your point will not be received. All animals, including humans, use eye contact to read intentions and many have said that the eyes are the windows to the soul. A strong gaze also captivates the audience. You demand attention by giving it."
~Heather Lyman

I'm so Excited

Let me give you an illustration showing the difference between our professional culture and others. Imagine you are about to teach a group of veteran officers (insert any topic here) and you jump up with your hands held high and say, *"I'm just so excited to be here today with all of you. I'm excited to get to know all of you and share this journey together. I want each of you to share your three favorite hobbies and the names of your pets."* You are now the most hated person in the room, and every cop is looking for the nearest escape route. This style may work great for sales and marketing groups, but not cops. Remember not to say *"I'm so excited,"* and you are already a better police instructor.

> Remember not to say *"I'm so excited,"* and you are already a better police instructor.

I have been fortunate (most of the time) to have attended training conferences on new and innovative learning methods outside the law enforcement community. I heard the magic words *"I'm so excited"* at every workshop, general session, and keynote address. Business, marketing, and education professionals have to be the most *excited* people I have ever seen. The phrase is still taught in public speaking classes but has been so abused that it feels fake when you hear it, even if it is true.

Professional speakers may be able to fake excitement with the average person, but you can't fool cops. They profile everyone they come in contact with and decide for themselves if the person is trustworthy, sincere, and passionate about the topic.

Start Out Slow and Small

Consider shadowing another instructor or co-teaching a class before going it alone. There are great websites – Ted.com and AmericanRhetoric.com – that offer you a ringside seat to great examples of public speaking. If you see something you like while watching a video, consider using it, and if a speaker has a trait you find annoying, forget it. Be on the lookout for ways to improve your craft. Concentrate on how each presenter delivers their message and if they are passionate about their subject. When you find a presenter who has a dynamic style of delivery, keep watching and figure out what makes it dynamic.

Consider speaking at a Toastmasters meeting. They offer a learn-by-doing workshop set in a friendly atmosphere. You can hone your speaking skills at one of their weekly, biweekly or monthly meetings (these generally last about an hour). There is no instructor; instead, the members evaluate one another. You can get real feedback before trying something new with a law enforcement audience. Find a local club by visiting Toastmasters.org.

Make it Personal

Assemble and arrange your experiences, thoughts, and ideas. List them at the end of each chapter. Include events or lessons you have learned as a cop, parent, spouse, or person. When you need a relevant experience for a talk, it will be easy to find. Include one of your experiences in *every* presentation you deliver. You can confidently talk about your experiences and that provides you with a comfortable format to start. Search for significant events that provided you with a life lesson that will benefit your audience as well.

Have a Conversation

We are social people at heart. If you wanted to teach your friend something new, you probably would not sit them in a classroom and start up a slide presentation. You would have a conversation with them explaining the information and how it would help them. A conversation is also the way you should communicate to your audience – talk to them like a friend. Our purpose in using slide shows, handouts, and group exercises is to help engage and add interest; however, these should never replace the conversation. *You* should be the main point of reference during the talk – not your slides.

> You should be the main point of reference during the talk – not your slides.

If you look up the word *talk* in a thesaurus, you will see *encounter* as a synonym. These are two-sided conversations where someone learns by experiencing something new. It is not defined as a monotone dissertation or one-sided lecture; nor should your presentation be. An encounter with your topic challenges your students to learn through involvement – not just sitting there. *Encounter* is also synonymous with *battle, clash, conflict, dispute, engagement,* and *quarrel.* We can create an *encounter* through group exercises that involve disputes and quarrels or by using stories with conflicts that cause clashes and engagement in the students' mind. An *encounter* is exactly what you want to provide. Would you rather an *encounter* the next time you are the student?

The opposite of *encounter* is *to avoid, evade,* or *run away.* That is what some instructors do when they stand behind the lectern and conduct a one-way talk. They appear to be hiding because they are; they feel safer by not allowing their students to be involved.

Even the topics that sound interesting to begin with (like *Firearms* or *Tactical Entry*) can lack a two-way conversation and the *encounter* students are seeking. *Yield* and *surrender* are also the opposites of *encounter,* and for our students to receive a dynamic presentation, we must never appear to *yield* or *surrender* to our anxiety, computer problems, or challenging questions. Be the unique instructor who has a conversation with your audience and they will *encounter* new information.

> *"It is not enough to fight. It is the spirit which we bring to the fight that decides the issue. It's morale that wins the victory."* ~George C. Marshall

Active Learning Creates Humor

The more active learning you build into your presentation, the more humor, interest, and engagement will be created. Group exercises, role-plays, demonstrations, and teach-backs are highly charged humor machines. Not only are these methods the best way to learn but they are inherently funny.

Studies show that cognitive thinking and creativity will dramatically increase with positive emotions, and humor is as positive as we get. If you feel comfortable, practice using humor in your presentations and look for the right anecdote, story, or example that fits. Humor helps the audience relax and connect to the presentation as well as the presenter. Everyone enjoys a lecture more when they get the chance to laugh and smile.

Try to Have Fun, Not be Funny

Funny stuff will happen whether you try for it or not. Enjoy the interaction and have *fun* every time you teach, but do not worry about being *funny*. When you enjoy training the class, they enjoy being trained; laughter will erupt eventually with that combination.

Using your natural humor during a presentation is a confidence builder that brings your topic alive. It is a common form of communication and comfortable for most police instructors to use. Cops are some of the funniest people I know, but don't try a stand-up comedy act. Use light hearted and relevant humor when telling stories, and realize that everyone is born with at least a little bit of *funny* in them.

Humor lightens up the tense subjects we must cover in law enforcement making learning more enjoyable, but we cannot plan for every event that might happen. I was teaching the block on *Crisis Intervention* when jack-hammering started on the roof above the classroom. I just laughed and said, *"I hope I didn't arrest one of those workers or this could be a long week for you guys."*

During the break I asked the crew how long their work would last. *"Every five minutes or so, we'll be hammering for a few seconds,"* the foreman responded. Not what I wanted to hear, but there was little else I could do. No other rooms were available, and it was a mandatory class for my audience.

It would not do any good to complain to the students (though I wanted to). Instead, I instructed them that each time the jack-hammering started, they were to write a short summary of the previous five minutes. Each time the hammering stopped a few students read their summaries to make sure the class understood the material. As it turned out, this worked great as a review method. It is better to laugh at those things that are beyond our control than to get angry and accomplish nothing. Take it from a Master Jedi.

"Anger leads to hate. Hate leads to suffering." ~Yoda

Humor Safety Valve

You can create a safety valve to use if a class does not laugh when you are trying to be funny. It builds confidence knowing that you are covered – and it works well with our dry cop humor.

When you are trying to be funny, or sneak a sly joke into your lesson, make sure you keep a straight face – pause for a moment and watch the reaction of your audience. *Only* after your audience starts smiling should you join them, but not before. If they do not acknowledge your attempt at humor simply move on like it was planned that way. It allows you an escape if your audience does not find you funny at the moment you thought they would.

If you decide to tell a joke (which I personally avoid doing) and it *bombs,* just own it. Say something self-deprecating, *"No wonder I'm a cop instead of a comic,"* or walk over to the lectern and act like you are crossing something off a list and say, *"I won't need that one again"* and the students *will* start laughing.

The worst response you can have is to blame the audience for not *getting* your humor. *"This is a rough crowd"* is an offensive comment coming from a presenter, and *"Come on guys that's my best material"* is a discouraging vision of what is still to come. You have just acknowledged that you were trying really hard to be funny and you suck at it. Statements like these would annoy anyone, and they will distance the audience from your message.

I thank my audience when I bomb by saying, *"My next class thanks you for your sacrifice, because they won't have to hear that."* It only deepens the respect from our class when we are honest and down to earth. It also makes it easier for us to take a risk the next time knowing we will survive.

Some Days Won't Be Funny

I recently used an anecdote that I had told dozens of times before. It was always met with big laughs, but on this occasion it fell flat. I was a little bewildered by the silence because it had never failed to get laughs before. I managed to use the *Humor Safety Valve* and moved on, but I was determined to find out what I did wrong.

There was nothing that would be funny to this class on that particular day. During the next break, I found out that one of the cadets in the class was upset because his best friend had committed suicide over night. He was having a personal crisis, and I had completely missed it – the rest of the class had not. I had been focused on my presentation instead of the audience. I quickly changed my focus and saw to the needs of the cadet before continuing on.

We may never know why a particular audience did not respond on a particular day as we thought they would, and that is just the way it is. We are there to teach more than to entertain, but it is nice when we can do both.

Keep it Clean

Do not use nasty or unprofessional humor. After all, it is not a *Comedy Central Roast*. I only mention this because I have seen it done. There are instructors who choose to use constant profanity and vulgar jokes. Some decide to use valuable training time as a personal soapbox to let the audience know how they are getting screwed.

A plethora of profanity does not sound professional coming from an instructor who represents the noble profession of law enforcement. I know I will have arguments with this point, and I must admit that I once found myself following the cop culture of believing *"Profanity is the only way to get some people's attention"* and *"It's the only language they understand."* Looking back, it should have made as much sense as a helicopter with ejector seats, but I bought into it because I wanted to. I eventually realized it was a crappy excuse to be belligerent, and I have not felt the need to use profanity even once since my rookie year.

I have served in several different environments, from the inner city to the suburbs, and I have investigated street gangs, predators, and murderers. Profanity is not necessary and should not be used by an instructor without a purpose. Like I said before, this is the *Richipedia* take on profanity, and you are free to chuck it if you like (trash the opinion – keep the book).

I would likely have carried on using profanity had it not been for the day my daughter, Nadia, repeated something I had said. I would like to say my Christian faith did it for me, but it was a three-year-old. It was an embarrassing way to be reminded that I served as an example for her as well as the community, and it

---

was not the example I wanted coming to mind when others thought of me or my profession. That was the last time I used profanity without some specific purpose and that decision has never hindered me as a cop or as an instructor.

"Men are like steel. When they lose their temper, they lose their worth." ~Chuck Norris

No One Really Cares If You Screw Up

The audience is on your side. They want you to do well and succeed as their instructor. No one wants to sit through a lousy presentation – they want you to be prepared, knowledgeable, and a little funny. It will not do you any good to worry about something going wrong; at some point, it will. Those are the moments when you can prove your worth to the audience by adapting to whatever happens.

> You are human – they are human – they understand. Cut yourself some slack.

If you screw something up, just keep moving. Make a quick joke about the blunder if you like, but don't worry about it. Some instructors become nervous because they think every audience has it in for them. They do not. You are human – they are human – they understand. Cut yourself some slack.

"Give me a productive error over a boring, mundane and unproductive fact any day." ~ Anonymous

I'm the Greatest Cop Ever!

That is the way I felt the first time I received an award as a cop. My *ego* had me wanting to scream, *"I'm the greatest cop in the universe"* as I threw my arms in the air, but common sense reminded me that it was a laminated board with a brass plate. The award was not special in itself, but it was refreshing that others thought I was a good officer. I soon found myself designing presentations for child safety, drug abuse, school violence, and a host of other topics. I used teenagers to help with the presentations that became so popular and successful that we ended up on a stage in front of 4,000 people. I looked out into the lights and saw an ocean of faces – I no longer felt like the greatest cop ever. Instead, I found myself nervous and a little worried.

I have presented to cops, cadets, and governors. I have addressed White House cabinet members, clubs, and parents. I have given speeches, designed workshops, and directed conferences. All those things prove absolutely *nothing* to my next audience. And I mean *nothing!* I still get nervous and I still worry that I may miss something important – even if the class has two students. I know they are counting on me to give them something worthwhile.

I have been blessed with awards and recognition, but there have been audiences throughout my career who were happy to see my presentations end. Those are the people who should be honored. For every award I received, a host of people suffered at my hands. They suffered through my trial and error period as I tried to understand learning theories and made adjustments.

I still find myself confused at times wondering what went wrong with a particular technique or presentation. My confusion now comes at a higher level and with the confidence that I will find opportunities through unexpected situations. Several of the ideas in this book came as the result of confusion, screw ups, and spontaneity.

There is no magic pixie dust or *7 secrets to success* for police instructors. This is not an infomercial promising you something that does not exist. However, you can use the techniques in *Police Instructor* to enhance your presentations. No one is the *greatest cop ever*, but in my humble opinion, we do serve the *greatest profession* on the planet.

> *"Character cannot be developed in ease and quiet.*
> *Only through experience of trial and suffering can the soul*
> *be strengthened, ambition inspired, and success*
> *achieved." ~Helen Keller*

Improve Your Mojo

People are not born great detectives, crime scene investigators, or cops. They may have God-given talents for our profession but it takes hard work to get in. Only through determination and training can cadets achieve a worthwhile career in law enforcement and gain the experience to become a great cop. It also takes education, training, and experience to become a great police instructor, and like any important law enforcement duty, the journey will involve some struggles. It is worth the effort to persevere and take your place as a trainer of guardians.

You should always look for that *"one more thing"* that will make you a better instructor. A new idea, unique activity, or innovative method that will provide you with cool *Ninja instructor skills* that no other trainer possesses. Then, you can be as cool as *SPIM*.

Seeking to improve will make you a good instructor. There is always some area where you can improve, and if you are already a *good* instructor, seeking to improve is how you become a *great* instructor.

Take one new idea from this book (or some other resource), and incorporate it into your next presentation – it will be more effective and engaging. Even better, add three or four ideas and make it intriguing. You will stand out with law enforcers and cadets by doing the little things that many instructors will not.

As you read through *Police Instructor,* consider your strengths and weaknesses and set a few new goals. Decide now which new *Ninja instructor skills* you will add to your next presentation. Refrain from being your own worst enemy and cut yourself some slack when it comes to trying something new. If it does not feel right, try something else – but keep trying. What really counts is your determination to continually improve your craft.

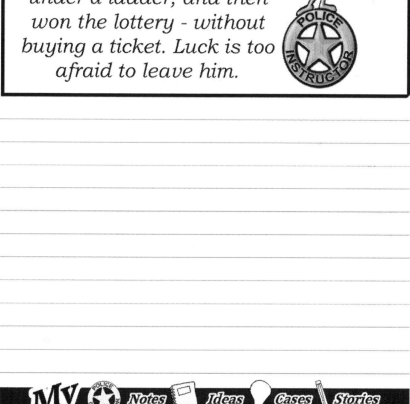

SPIM Factoid

SPIM smashed a mirror over a black cat while standing under a ladder, and then won the lottery - without buying a ticket. Luck is too afraid to leave him.

Cadet Stewart

Disruptive Cops & Challenging Cadets

I felt the hair rising on the back of my neck. Fear and anxiety were having an effect on my presentation. I knew Stewart would have his hand up again and pose another meaningless question. As I continued teaching, I noticed the other students looking with disgust in Stewart's direction. He couldn't wait for me to turn around and finally interrupted, *"Officer Neil, I have another question."* This was dangerous ground to stand on. He could go on for several minutes giving his viewpoint which rarely had anything to do with our topic. He rarely had a question – just opinions. The class was upset with him for droning on about nothing, and they were becoming equally as upset with me for allowing it to happen.

Stewart was in his late thirties and trying to change careers, but he was insecure about life and tried to prove himself more

---

intelligent than his younger classmates. He annoyed the other cadets and every instructor who taught him. During breaks, he would come up and whisper comments about his vast knowledge of law enforcement to me (obviously obtained from watching *T.J. Hooker*). The Stewarts of the world can become a problem for you as an instructor. They are known by teachers and public speakers as a *stage hog*, and they are determined to have everyone listen to their endless nonsense. The nickname *stage hog* is contradictory since these people should never be on stage – ever! If you allow them to continue with irrelevant questions and off-topic comments, your class will blame you.

> If you allow them to continue with irrelevant questions and off-topic comments, your class will blame you.

You have to act early and discourage students from competing for time through rules or other methods. This is law enforcement and not a fifth grade classroom where you need to be politically correct every time you handle a disruption. Be as professional as you can, but in the end, make sure you are in control of the class. I used several of the following methods with Stewart and others just like him, and I hope you will find them useful when confronted with a disruptive student of your own.

"He who angers you conquers you." ~Elizabeth Kenny

Move Toward the Talker

This one comes naturally to most educators. If you walk toward a student who is talking, they will abruptly stop. If you move around the room like I do, it is a natural and effective method, and you don't need to stop your presentation to deal with the interruption. It works with the cadet texting under the table, a pair whispering back and forth, or someone starting to doze off. It usually gets their attention back on you and the presentation. If you currently do not move around the room, this technique gives you another reason to start.

Rolling the Dice

Rolling the Dice is an effective method of calling on a student when no one seems interested in volunteering an answer. It also cuts down dramatically on the *stage hog* in your class by randomly selecting the cadet when a question arises.

There are several reasons to use dice but I started for only one. I wanted more student participation. I wanted to avoid creating passive students who were afraid to volunteer or answer a question. I originally started with the idea of using just one, but I now have a polyhedral 7 dice set. It sounds impressive, but it only costs five dollars from Amazon. The dice set normally comes with 10-, 12-, and 20-sided dice. They will cover the size of most classes, but 30-sided dice are available as well for another two dollars.

When a question is posed during your presentation, leave it to chance to see who will be answering. Assign a number to each student, and if the dice lands on that number, they are chosen – it's that simple. It takes away the *over-eager* student who wants to answer everything as well as the student who avoids eye contact at all costs. It creates anticipation (I did not originally foresee) for the class, and to add some fun and drama, I have the students take turns rolling the dice. They have the fate of their classmates in their hands, and they like it.

You can add another component to the activity when a cadet answers incorrectly. Let them roll one of the dice to determine how many pushups, sit-ups, or leg scissors they have to do for missing the question. The one who answered wrong and the student who rolled the dice that chose them are in it together. Everyone is more attentive when their classmates can be affected by their participation in the class.

The random selection is unique and it keeps their attention on the presentation. Cadets like anything that keeps discussions from being dominated by a few students, and I find students are now looking forward to the dice coming out of my backpack. I do not have any research to tell you why it works so well – but it does.

The technique will solicit more wrong answers from the class at first, but you will find the wrong answers lead to better discussions and uncover confusion about your topic that might not have been volunteered otherwise. This is a winning combination for a police instructor.

You can use the dice for other decisions as well – be creative. If you are using a group exercise, have each of them roll the dice to see who will be in charge. That way it always changes, and the same *stage hog* will not take over each time they are in a group. The dice are also available in 100-sided if you find the need and are a cheap investment for such an effective learning tool.

Disruptions Will Cause a Late Departure

Place the responsibility on your disruptive student for delaying others by saying, *"I have a lot to cover, and if we are going to get out of here on time we need to stay on topic. If you have other questions or comments, I will be happy to stay after class to help you."* With the rest of the class staring at the *stage hog,* they will feel the pressure to stop interrupting your presentation.

They are rarely confused and just want a platform to talk but not enough to make the rest of the class mad at them. The technique works well and they never stay after to ask you anything – if they do – it is only your time they are wasting; the class will appreciate your sacrifice.

The 20-Second Inquiry

I developed *The 20-Second Inquiry* after many run-ins with the Stewarts of the world. It will prevent long-winded questions and cadets who want the spotlight. It will also stop those who ponder out loud instead of thinking of what to ask ahead of time. Here is how I instruct my audience using *The 20-Second Inquiry*:

I want you all to ask questions so you understand what we cover together, but as police officers you will need to think before asking questions of others. Thinking first will ensure you have asked the appropriate question of a victim, witness, or suspect. If you ask long-winded questions, they become confusing and might be misunderstood.

Before you ask a question, I want you to think about how to ask it effectively. This will make the question clear in your mind and keep the class on topic. You will have 20 seconds to get your question asked once I call on you, and your classmates will watch the time to keep you honest. If it is not related to the subject, wait until the break to ask it.

Keep the rule light hearted so your students see it as a benefit and not a punishment. They *will* actually time each other and joke around when a cadet gets long-winded or asks a confusing question. They buy into the idea, and it really does help them to formulate better questions. The skill will benefit them throughout the academy and their career. I admit that was not my original concern but it is a definite plus. It has evolved from a rule into a learning method.

As an added component, you can see if the students can answer each other's questions. It is a quick test to see if everyone is lost or just the student asking the question.

Leave a Note

Provide your students with index cards and instruct them to write down their questions. Tell them, if a question comes to mind but it is off topic, write it down. If the question is about the section we covered 20 minutes ago, write it down. If you feel embarrassed to ask the question in front of the others, write it down.

Have your students leave the questions on the lectern at break time, and then answer them when they return or at the end of the day. The questions get answered for everyone, and the student who wants to remain anonymous does. I have found that the anonymous questions can be some of the most insightful.

Question Board

Have a designated question board in the classroom. Advise your audience to write their questions on the white board (or chalk board if you're old-school) during the break. If other students have the same question, instruct them to place a checkmark next to it. It serves as a quick method to see if your class is struggling with the material, and it encourages students to discuss the information during the breaks once they realize they are not alone.

The technique shows the audience that you are interested in helping them learn. The *Question Board* and *Leave a Note* both help you keep the natural flow of your presentation from unnecessary interruptions.

Pull the Stage Hog In

Yes, that is exactly what I meant to say. If nothing else is working, you can pull the *stage hog* into your presentation. If you are teaching a class with a *stage hog* who is constantly interrupting, you must do something quickly. There is not always enough time to use other (more polite) techniques. Pulling them deeper into your presentation can be an effective technique to avoid further disruption and possible confrontations.

I understand that it sounds a little crazy but it works with this type of person. If the *stage hog* wants the attention, give it to them with greater intensity. The following is just an example to give you an idea of what I mean. I will use Stewart as my example. Imagine that he has been continually interrupting my class from the start. Here is how I can pull him in, and shut him down.

"I imagine Stewart would handle this situation differently; how about it, Stewart? Hold on. Hey Stewart, do you have a different opinion on this? Wait a minute. Let's give Stewart the opportunity to answer the question. I am sure he will know."

Stewart will do everything that he can to shrink into the corner, and he won't be a *stage hog* the rest of the day. You will see his body language change; he will start to look like a suspect squirming in the chair of an interrogation room. It is only fun for the *stage hog* when they grab the spotlight – not when you shine it on them.

Do Not Focus on Minor Distractions

If you are giving a presentation to a large group, you have less control than in a classroom of cadets. We want an audience that knows what *polite* means, but we do not always get it. We want the crowd to laugh at our jokes, be swayed by our knowledge of the material, and turn off their cell phones. We are competing with an entertaining world that may be more important to the audience than our presentation. Don't worry about it.

With a big crowd, you cannot worry about one person who is distracted. Your focus should be on those who are paying attention. If an audience member is whispering to a neighbor or playing with their cell phone and no one else cares – why should you? Give the people who are paying attention everything you have, and forget about the others.

"Speak when you are angry and you will make the best speech you will ever regret." ~Ambrose Bierce

Challenging Rooms and Venues

The room can be as much an interruption as an arrogant student. Some rooms are horrid for a presentation or conducting a police academy class. It can be like having a funeral at *Chuck E. Cheese's*. There are better venues, but you do not always have a choice when it comes to location.

I have had jack-hammering on the roof above my classroom and broken thermostats that raised the temperature to 80 degrees. All you can do is your best. Think of a creative way to deal with the space you are given and show the audience how to adapt and overcome a difficult situation.

Just recently, I was teaching an evening class on *Child Abuse and Neglect Investigation* and a storm knocked out the electricity; down went my slide show with the lights. The common grimaces and complaints were heard from the students along with *"I guess that's it."* I said *"Not a chance, you have flashlights, so use them."* They just laughed – it was not dark yet but it soon would be. *"That sucks,"* was the thought going through my mind. I taught the subject many times before and had developed several group exercises (illustrated later in the book) to use with it. I simply changed my agenda and used the group exercises while we were without power. It pays to plan ahead for these situations since you never know what will happen to disrupt your presentation.

Another recent issue with a room was my own blunder. I was teaching an in-service program on search methods for a *Child Abduction Response Team*. I have a great slide show with maps and resources to train these groups, and I *assumed* it would work with any layout. I was wrong. The group met in a city council facility with flat screen televisions mounted at one end of the room, but the audience sat 40 feet away. My slides could not have been viewed with binoculars.

I had never run into such a situation, and I did not check the room out in advance like I should have. I asked the group to stand in the front of the room where they could see, and even then, some of the images were too small. Fortunately, I had detailed handouts for them to look at when they could not see the images on the screen, and it worked out in the end. If you are teaching somewhere for the first time, do some scouting and make sure you understand the possible complications.

If you complain about the room, your audience will focus on that instead of your presentation, and no one will learn. Do the best you can with what you have, and model how to deal with the unexpected for your students.

> *"People who fly into a rage always make a bad landing."*
> *~Will Rogers*

Veterans & Experts in Your Class

Most veterans who are a disruption to your class can be convinced to cooperate just by giving them something of value for their time, and if not, pull them to the side and have a respectful but direct conversation. Thank them for their input, acknowledge their contribution, and ask that additional comments be saved for afterwards. If they cannot cooperate, they should be asked to leave like anyone else.

Another challenging situation is presented when a student in your class possesses more experience or expertise than you – especially on the topic you are teaching. This is only a problem if you ignore the student and the wisdom they can bring to your class.

I recently taught a basic academy class that had three veteran officers from different states. They were each required to complete the *Ohio Revised Code* section of the legal block to meet the certification requirements for the state. They each added veteran insights on the elements of the crimes as we moved through the statutes, and I made sure of it by asking them to participate. I wanted their experience to be a benefit for my cadets, and it was.

The most interesting of the three was a recent transfer from Maine. He was actually the Chief of Police for Portland and the soon to be Chief of Police for Cincinnati, Ohio. Chief Craig started his career with the Detroit Police Department in 1977 (I was in elementary school at the time) and moved to the LAPD in 1981. He spent 28 years in Los Angeles and rose to the rank of Captain III. From 2002 to 2009, he served as the Commanding Officer of the West, Southwest, and Southeast areas of the city. From there he went to Portland, Maine and then ended up in the Buckeye State. That is quite a résumé.

I was covering *Crimes Against the Public Peace* and had an officer who served during the L.A. riots in my class. I could not have hoped for a better guest speaker for my cadets. He graciously gave them examples that coincided with the elements they were learning. It would have been inexcusable for me not to involve him and the other veteran officers in the learning process.

The worst thing you can do is ignore these people in your class. Let them know before you start that you would like to call on them for input. If they just want to sit in the back of the room and be left alone – so be it, but most are happy to help out.

Earn Their Respect

When a class does not respect the instructor, they are much more likely to be disruptive and disrespectful. Make sure you do not add to the problem by losing their respect with a lack of preparation or a bad attitude.

It is usually one of three things that will cost you the respect of a law enforcement audience:

1. You come to class unprepared and it shows through your talk, handouts, and slides. It is okay to be nervous; students will not care as long as they get some value for their time. But if you have nothing that resembles useful information, it is unforgivable in our profession.

2. You act as if you are the greatest cop in the universe and the class should form a fan club. You talk about every certificate you have and use every cop cliché claiming they are based on your life. The only class discussion will be, *"How did this guy become an instructor?"*

3. The fastest way to lose all respect and credibility is to lie. And I mean lie about anything, regardless of its importance. An instructor knowingly lies and thinks no one in the class will notice. Instead of just saying the magic words, *"I don't know the answer to that"* they lie to look smarter. They not only look stupid but have become so. Their ego will not allow them to admit that they don't know everything about the topic, and the class treats them like a *perp* instead of an instructor – and they should.

SPIM Factoid
The wolverine is extinct in most of America because SPIM is an Ohio State Buckeye!

Dynamic Delivery

Your audience wants an instructor who not only believes in what they are saying but one who has confidence in their ability to present it well. Do not diminish their belief and be *kind of* bold – be bold! Not cocky or arrogant, but bold in the knowledge that you have value to offer through your experience and preparation. A dynamic presentation is lean and confident. It does not require repetitive material that fluffs it up but stays lean by offering wisdom over fluff.

A dynamic police instructor will see their audience as *guardians of justice* and train them for that mission. They will not use the techniques and methods throughout this book as a cosmetic fix for their presentations but recognize the human element as the most important ingredient in learning. It is an element sometimes lost and replaced by cookie cutter slide show presentations. Instead of following a failed system, you can engage your audience by providing them with realities and relevant active learning techniques like those illustrated in *Police Instructor.*

The Ten Minute Rule

This is a strategy that I believe in so much that every slide presentation I have is set up paying respect to it; it can help you keep the attention level high with any audience.

Boring cop classes are easy to come by, and like you, I have attended a few that could have served as anesthesia. In a study from the 70's, the U.S. Navy indicated an attention span of 18 minutes was the most you could expect without changing something in a presentation. Dr. John Medina, an award winning teacher, points to his research that shows the span is now down to 10 minutes. It comes as little surprise considering how many distractions we are competing against today as instructors. If I find myself in a boring class, I am more drawn (against

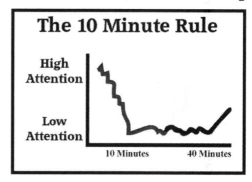

my will) to my *Android* than the instructor. When you build variety into your presentation, you will not be competing for the attention of your audience – it will be on you.

Some topic areas in the basic academy are lengthy – *Community Diversity* is a 24-hour block – but you can still set up your presentation using *The 10 Minute Rule.* It does not require a change of topics, just a change in the way you are currently teaching the topic.

Here are some ideas that will provide a change in the learning environment using the rule:

☆ Have a picture of the 2001 Cincinnati race riots on the screen and change gears from the SPO on race relations to the aftermath when they fail.

* Go back to teaching your SPO for ten minutes, and then stop and assign a group exercise on values. Allow students to compare their top five beliefs with the others in the class.
* Teach for another 10 minutes using your prepared slides, and then stop and show a video on the Islamic Faith.
* After another 10 minutes of teaching goes by, tell the story of *Silvestre S. Herrera* – a WWII *hero* who won the *Congressional Medal of Honor* – though he was not a U.S. citizen.
* Go another 10 minutes and display a picture of the one dollar bill. Ask the audience if they know why the *Star of David* is located above the eagle, or if they know who *Haym Solomon* was.
* Go another 10 minutes and play the news coverage of *Sgt. Crawley's* arrest of Harvard Professor *Henry Gates Jr.* for the class (that is always a lively discussion).
* After 10 more minutes of teaching, ask them what ethnicity was predominate with the first *American* law enforcement officers, and why they were picked for the job.

It really is that easy to lay out your presentation using *The Ten Minute Rule*. I can go on and on because those are the actual items I have in my presentation for *Community Diversity*. It can be time-consuming work when you first follow this principle, but it is well worth it when you consider who we are training.

You feel good as an instructor when your presentation has the appreciation of your class. They will welcome the journey that this type of training takes them on, and you will be welcomed back – *"We're glad we have you tonight!"*

The ideas used in the previous example are not hard to find, and they add great interest to any presentation. Cadets do not need long lists from a curriculum to be professional law enforcement officers. They need knowledge based on real life experiences provided by *you* through different types of visual media and stories. Make it your mission to give them something new, however small it may be, every *10* minutes or so.

Introduce *You* Not Your Title

"Why am I here today? It all started with a tackle that could have been an ESPN highlight – if I had not landed on a parking block. A smarter cop would have waited until the grass and then tackled the bad guy to cushion the fall. The concrete block shoved my ribs into my spinal cord causing permanent damage. I now have 2 battery packs in my back, and they power 4 wires that carry electricity to my spinal cord – much like a Taser. I even recharge myself like a robot by plugging into an outlet. I wanted to be R2D2 when I was a kid, so I finally got my wish - batteries, wires, and all.

The man who blessed me with my Star Wars persona was wanted for a minor traffic violation, but he fought like he had just committed murder. Unlike those of you here today, I can no longer meet the physical demands law enforcement places on a body. I consider myself fortunate to be able to use the knowledge I gained through my experiences to serve you as an instructor. I still do my part to protect and serve our society by training you – the future guardians of justice. Now let's get started and we will find out more about each other as we move through this topic together."

This introduction takes me less than two minutes to present to a new class. It is not my police biography, a list of achievements, or my entire repertoire. It is a story that engages the listener with a quick glimpse of who I am. It leaves them wanting to know more about my police experience, and that is a good thing. I let the audience know that I will be personal with them encouraging them to be personal with me.

Do not try to memorize a particular opening or use the same one every time, and avoid the boring format most instructors adopt. They spend several minutes going through their résumé and list of certificates, or worse, they get on a soap box for the first fifteen minutes of class. I have tried these methods and gained nothing but contempt from my audience.

Leave the *"old and busted"* format behind, and introduce yourself as you would when meeting someone new. Take the opportunity and capture the interest of your audience right from the start.

"It's so much easier to pray for a bore than to go and see one." ~C. S. Lewis

First Impressions

First impressions are big in the world of law enforcement, and it starts when you arrive in the room. Make sure you get there early and set up with time to spare. It is annoying when an instructor spends the first ten minutes messing around with the computer. It will not impress your audience if you act like their time is not as valuable as yours.

Be straightforward and show the audience respect, and they will do the same for you. Express your honest opinions without reservation and the audience will feel connected with your message even if they disagree with you. It is important that the audience understands you are there to talk *with* them, not *at* them. You are there to have a conversation and challenge them to participate. Here are a few easy ways to connect with any audience:

* **Mention people.** Before you start speaking, meet the people who are there to hear your presentation. Ask them questions about work, family, and what they hope to get from your talk. Once you start, strategically weave a few of the names and interesting bits of information you discovered into your message.

* **Mention groups.** Along with mentioning people, you can talk about what affects the group. If it's an academy class, speak about their commander (*always* in a good light), joke about push-ups, or other things they have in common. If you are presenting to another group, find out as much as you can about them through their website or by talking to some of the members. Mention traits, ideas, or struggles shared by the group.

* **Ask questions.** Instead of simply transferring information during your presentation, include the audience by asking questions – not just the *yes* or *no* type. Invite them to share their ideas, opinions, stories, and reactions.

* **Current & local news.** Check for relevant news that is hot off the presses. With a multitude of law enforcement websites, it is easy for you to get the most up-to-date

information available on any subject. Check the local newspaper or websites for relevant information specific to your training location. It adds freshness when you talk about current events happening in the lives of your audience.

★ **Customize the show.** It can add a connection simply by customizing your first slide with a logo, badge, or patch that represents the audience. You may also find a place to slip other types of news or information into your presentation that will directly relate to the group.

"All learning is experience. Everything else is just information." ~Albert Einstein.

Please No, Not the Notes!

Notes are to serve as a quick reference, and the same concept should apply to your slide show. Know your material well enough that a quick look will remind you of the material. It is *you* who must train the class not your slides, notes, or lesson plan.

Do not read off the curriculum like it is a book. My most painful memories from the police academy are of instructors who simply read the lesson plan aloud – I almost became a fireman (not really, I'm just trying to add some drama). Equally as important – do not read your slides to the class or have them read the slides to you.

Having students read slides has been added as a useful technique by some instructors. The concept of involving the students in the learning process makes sense, but the technique is not one that students enjoy. On one survey, cadets from three different academies indicated that the technique was one of the most annoying methods instructors used. It was not even an option on the survey, and it still managed to make it to the top of the list as a *write in.* They do not like it.

I would suggest only using the method when you have a specific purpose in mind. If you have a story for a group exercise, you may have one of the students read the slide for the class. The technique can work well in such a manner, but if a slide is filled with bullet points, reconsider having anyone read it – including you. It will serve no purpose but to fill time and annoy your audience. Fill their time with group exercises and active learning methods instead.

Use Your Voice

Let your tone of voice vary naturally during your presentation just as it does when you have a conversation with a friend. When making an important point, use a stronger tone or more rapid pace. If you are telling a story of an arrest, use your voice to express the tension of the encounter. Make the motions with your hands as if you are wrestling the suspect to the ground and shout out the commands, *"Stop resisting, you're under arrest."* Your variety of tone, and pace, can add interest that grabs the audience's attention.

You should include pauses when you speak. It is far better to pause than respond with an *"uhh"* or *"uhm,"* but when we incorporate silence into our presentation, it always feels longer than it really is. The audience does not notice when you pause because they are taking that time to think about the material you have been covering. Imagine reading this book with no pauses – represented by periods and paragraphs. It would be a pain, and you would stop reading before finishing the first page. Your audience will stop listening in the same way if you fail to provide pauses between key points and stories.

Silence also serves to build a natural anticipation with the audience, and a long pause fills the room with silent interest that will pull them forward in their chairs wanting to know what comes next. If you fail to slow down, they never have enough time to concentrate on the information let alone be filled with anticipation.

Researchers have discovered that the use of vocal variety during your presentation can impact the heart rate of your audience. How powerful is that? Just by changing the volume of your voice, you create interest for your students. Speaking loudly might convey excitement or an important point on officer survival while using a soft voice might convey the sadness or

> Researchers have discovered that the use of vocal variety during your presentation can impact the heart rate of your audience.

compassion required when dealing with a rape victim.

Pace is the rate at which you speak, and varying it can add as much intrigue as your tone. If you are nervous, you will most likely speak too fast; watch yourself and slow down when necessary. The effects generated with a variable pace can be compelling. Speeding up can heighten the emotions in a dramatic situation involving a pursuit. Slowing down can create a greater impact when pointing out how many officers are killed during high-speed collisions.

Any time you use an important word or phrase slow down and change your pitch. For example, if you are teaching *Search and Seizure* use the technique to express words like *"reasonable"* or *"probable cause"* or *"totality of the circumstances."* You want your students to remember these key phrases throughout their careers. Focus their interest on these words through your slide design, voice, and gestures.

One of the best ways to bring out a dramatic voice is to use dramatic gestures, particularly facial gestures. When you are distinct with your face and other gestures, your voice tends to naturally match them. Be expressive, but be yourself when doing it. Your voice is the most valuable tool you have for a dynamic delivery, and learning new ways to use it will enhance your presentations.

Gestures Create Dynamic Connections

With much of our understanding coming visually, body language says a lot about a person. The key to using gestures is to keep them clear and natural. Use your hands naturally as if telling your kids a bedtime story – don't let them dangle at your sides or hide in your pockets. You also do not want to come off like a politician – most of them look like they are conducting a symphony orchestra.

There are too many contradictory rules when it comes to using gestures. One expert says to hold still and use minor hand movements, and another instructs us to act like we are in a theatrical production. Do not try to mimic gestures found in a book or on a website – that is not who you are, and you should not try to be someone you are not. If you follow crazy rules for gesturing, it will read as phony to law enforcers.

You can develop different movements to add realism to your stories. If you are talking about chasing a suspect, you can make a gesture as if you are running after him. You may describe grabbing the subject by making a motion with your hands as if you are reaching for his shoulders. A little acting adds to a dynamic presentation, but you are not competing for *Best Actor*.

Move Around the Room

Always use a remote for your slide show. It allows you to move freely around the room and have a conversation with the entire class. If the academy does not have a remote – buy one. You can purchase a good remote for $30, so there is no reason not to have one. A remote with more features can be purchased at a higher price, but a less expensive model will work well for most police instructors.

On top of moving your slide show forward, a remote can blank the screen, control the volume, and point with the built-in laser. Newer models use radio waves and eliminate the need to have a direct line of sight back to your computer allowing you to move freely around the room.

When you move around naturally it projects confidence to the audience and compels them to be attentive. You can make a strong point with your audience by moving toward them as you speak.

In my survey of police cadets, they identified *teaching from behind a desk* as one of the most annoying traits for an instructor. They also listed *constantly standing behind, or leaning on a lectern,* as unprofessional. Avoid these pitfalls by moving around, and your audience will become interested in your message.

~~Never~~ Turn Your Back on the Audience

I was waiting for the firing squad to pull the trigger as I covered the ruling from *Arizona v. Gant* just released by the U.S. Supreme Court. You would have thought I kicked a puppy in front of a class of first graders. The impact of the ruling was blown out of proportion, but it did not matter on that day – the audience was mad.

My instincts were to plead, *"Guys I'm one of you – don't get mad at me. It's not my fault!"* I fought the urge. Instead, I walked into the center of the class squeezing between the tables. I paused for a moment as everyone looked my way and said, *"Yeah, that's better."*

A veteran officer gruffly asked *"What in the hell are you doing?"* I replied back, *"It feels much safer out here with you guys than it does up there. I was waiting for one of you to blindfold me and give me a cigarette."* They all started laughing and the rule of never turning your back on the audience was thrown out of my repertoire for good.

> Do not let any rule define how you present your topic.

Violating the grand-daddy of all the *don'ts* in public speaking can be scary. I agree that it is best not to be up in front of the class with your back to everyone, but do not let any rule define how you present your topic. When I want a class to know *"we are in this thing together,"* I walk into the middle of the room among the students, and turn to look at the screen. Now as part of the audience, and with my back visible to a few, I point to the screen and assure them they are not alone in dealing with the topic at hand. I try not to stand right in front of anyone, but I do not want to be in the back of the room where no one can see me. Part of the secret is gaining physical and emotional distance from the information displayed on the screen and becoming part of the group again.

When the audience is mad at you (usually over the material you are covering), walking into the crowd and turning your back on them can work great. Teaching the legal requirements on *Use of Force* can turn heated when you cover controversial rulings. They want a lawyer or judge to be mad at but you are the one in front of the class. Get your classes fired up and allow them to argue their point and show frustration with a decision, but you will need to move on at some point, and that is where this technique comes in.

Slowly walk out into the center of the group and turn. Remind them *"I have the same frustrations guys. The people who hand* down such decisions have no idea what it is like for us to carry them out. I know we don't like this particular ruling but is everyone ready to move on?" There is a connection that comes from the technique that I cannot explain, and they always nod in appreciation for letting them vent. It is up to us to be engaging when the information we are presenting is not.

Take a Ride on the *The Beast*

When you are natural and honest during your presentation, the audience will let down their guard and that is when you attack! Holster your *Taser* and stay with me while I explain.

A good presenter (especially a motivational speaker) will pull their audience in and get them to relax. Then, they suddenly grab them with a sobering story or statistic that hits hard – upsetting some and weighing on others. Just as the crowd is about to yell at the speaker, they use humor or an inspirational tale that counteracts their mood. As the people begin to relax back in their seats, the presenter causes another conflict drawing them deeper into the talk. They want to jump up and speak their mind on the matter. They disagree!

A good speaker will use this method repeatedly throughout a presentation and eventually end on a motivational high note. Law enforcers are engaged by rapidly changing situations and will be compelled to interact when you use this technique.

I nicknamed this method *The Beast* after my favorite wooden roller coaster at the Kings Island Amusement Park in Ohio. The coaster is a rough and wild ride that causes each rider to question their decision to get on it. That is the same feeling we  are after when using *The Beast* to keep students engaged. They will always remember the experience and the material covered after a wild ride.

Let's make *Use of Force* our topic example. Begin with the Ninth Circuit Court of Appeals ruling that police officers were liable for the injuries caused when an uncooperative man hit the ground after being tased. The controversial decision upsets cadets when they hear that the subject was refusing to cooperate with police before he was tased, and the officers followed proper procedure. The court demanded there be an obvious danger to officers before they deploy a Taser, not just resistance. As the instructor, you should *lean* to the side of the court to incite the audience (even though you do not agree with the decision).

When you feel the time is right, calm them down by citing *Ohio's* sovereign immunity statute (2744.03 ORC). The state law provides immunity to officers from civil suits for injuries they cause others in the line of duty. Your students will be celebrating that they are not serving in the 9th Circuit, but in Ohio where they have *complete* immunity. Of course that is not true, they will never have *complete* immunity but let them stay up on their pedestal for a little while longer.

> Your students will be celebrating that they are not serving in the 9th Circuit, but in Ohio where they have *complete* immunity.

Provide them with the case of *Smith v. Freland* – a 1992 6th Circuit ruling that found in favor of a Springdale, Ohio officer who shot and killed a suspect who at the time was driving around him but had already shown he was a serious threat to society. Now the students are even more excited about being from the Buckeye State – do not leave them there for long.

Your next slide will simply have *"1983"* in big bold numbers (the number alone will bring down the spirits of most veteran cops). Explain how officers can be convicted of federal civil rights violations under 42 U.S.C. §1983 if their force is found to be excessive, and remind them of the 4 officers involved in the *Rodney King* beating by showing the video footage. Tell them how the officers were acquitted in a local Common Pleas Court but later convicted in Federal Court – cops can go to prison too! That will bring them back down from their *high* and into an argumentative state of mind.

Now provide them with the true test on use of force, the 1989 ruling of *Graham v. Conner* from the U.S. Supreme Court. The only word on the screen at this point will be *"Reasonable."* You want the class to absorb the word and the concept behind it.

The Beast is extremely effective with the *Type A* extroverts we train every day. Our learners become fully invested in the presentation when they find a point of contention. If they take the time to disagree with you, they are not sleeping, bored, or texting their friends. They are learning and building confidence by discussing hard topics openly with the group. *The Beast* is even better when combined with a *theme* in your presentation. Each of our previous examples could point back to the theme of *"Just be Reasonable."* Your audience may not remember every case law regarding the use of force but they will remember to *"Just be Reasonable."* The method will empower them to recall important information through an emotional encounter.

> *The Beast – When a police instructor takes their audience*
> *on an emotional roller coaster ride to create interest and*
> *encourage understanding. ~Richipedia*
> *[Just in case someone needs a quote for their thesis...]*

Prepare them Emotionally

We have shown our ability to prepare officers to physically perform their duties for years, but we must also prepare them emotionally for what will come. This is one area in which we are lacking at the academy and in-service training levels.

One academy requires students to wear a red sweat band on the wrist of their gun hand as a reminder to keep it *free*. Details like this serve as a constant reminder when you incorporate them with other topics. I exploit the wrist band by connecting real life examples of officers killed in the line of duty. I use video examples of officers making traffic stops with their flashlight in their gun hand only to be shot before they could draw their weapon. I also use photos from time to time. A cop with his hands in his pockets while interviewing a suspect or carrying a ticket book in his gun hand. This makes the wrist band a reality check each time they put it on. It has an emotional connection to the material in my presentation, and that creates a long term memory for them to build upon.

Police Instructor © 2011

Videos Provide Dynamic Involvement

Videos bring reality into your presentation but you should rarely let a video run through uninterrupted. Stop your video at key points and ask the audience to make the decision for the officer involved. Then play it through so they can see the actual outcome. Asking questions will force the students to make a decision before they see the final result – whether it was good or bad. Ask them, *"What do you see happening?" "Is the officer controlling the situation?" "Were there any mistakes made?" "What would you do in this situation?" "What sticks out to you about the people involved?"*

After the video is finished, go over the answers given by your students and compare them with the real outcome. Remind your audience that the officer on the video had to make the difficult decision without the benefit of *20/20* hindsight. If the cop messed up ask them, *"Is there any possibility you may have made the same mistake given the circumstance?"* It helps our learners to realize what a *rapidly evolving* situation looks like, and to understand the stress under which they will have to make similar decisions. You may decide to let the video play completely through the second time without interruption. It shows cadets how quickly decisions are made in the field.

If we allow students to passively watch our videos, they will be entertained but only slightly educated. When you pull them into the situation by asking difficult questions they become engaged, and they take away a little of your wisdom from the experience.

I am convinced that videos provide cops and cadets with a greater awareness of their skills and abilities that a basic lecture cannot. Such awareness will increase their survivability and teach them to trust their God-given intuition in similar situations.

Use Unique Videos

Consider using videos from television shows, news programs, and movies that provide relevance. The more unique, the more

---

they will remember the lesson connected to it. If you are teaching the *Interview and Interrogation* topic, you could start by using the opening scene from *The Wizard of Oz*.

In the scene, Dorothy runs away from home and stumbles into Professor Marvel and immediately feels connected to him. He notices her suitcase and predicts she is running away. *"How did you guess?"* she asks. But instead of answering, he predicts why she is running away, *"They don't understand you at home!"* Dorothy is amazed and says, *"Why, it's just like you could read what was inside me!"*

Professor Marvel connected with Dorothy by mentioning personal facts about her and showing an interest in her feelings. He gained her trust by building rapport. Law enforcers should use the same method when interviewing a victim, suspect, or witness.

You would still want to use videos of real police interrogations, but your audience will always remember the unique clip of Dorothy and Professor Marvel. The video is memorable, and more importantly, it will help you make an important point from the very beginning.

Next time you watch your favorite show look for moments that could be unique lessons for a future audience. Do not try to make every point using this technique but see the value it offers in the right situation.

Flip Charts are Dynamic

The flip chart has become extinct in many classrooms, but it is still a flexible and useful tool for teaching. It can help you facilitate group discussions, make important points, and break the addiction to PowerPoint presentations. Here are the tips, tricks, and rules that I have found useful when using a flip chart as a learning tool:

* Simplicity is the key. Do not clutter a flip chart page. Be concise and make sure your writing and drawings are legible from anywhere in the room. Use only one idea or concept on a page.
* Take your time and write – then talk. Your back is temporarily to the class and they cannot hear you well, so wait.
* Use block letters and make them at least 3 inches tall.

* Draw bullet points to indicate a new item. Dots, stars, squares, or whatever comes to mind will work.
* Use different colors to draw attention to a word or phrase. Use a different color for bullet points and illustrations, but use no more than three complementary colors on one page.

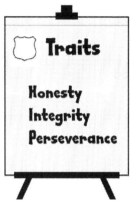

* Page titles should be larger than what follows below them. Consider using a different color marker for contrast or highlight the title by drawing a box around it.
* Leave the bottom 1/3 of the page blank so you do not have to crouch down and write on it. If you need the space, you can lift several pages up to a position where you can comfortably write on them. You can also kneel down or pull a chair up to the easel so you can write on the bottom, but I find it easier to just leave it blank.
* Write your notes in the top corners of each page using a light colored pencil. The audience will not be able to see the writing and it allows you to continue on without looking at your slide show, lesson plan, or notes.
* Save space by replacing words (like *money)* with symbols (like $). Instead of *probable cause* write *PC, law enforcement officer* becomes *LEO, disorderly conduct* is *DC,* and so on.
* If the flip chart is blank, you can add lines with a pencil and yard stick. Use faint lines 4 to 5 inches apart to allow for large letters.
* Use all capital letters for your titles and lower case for everything else on the page.

There is a multitude of ways to incorporate flip charts into your presentation; these are some of the techniques you may find useful as a police instructor:
* Flip charts should always be part of your back-up plan if the power goes out (and it will go out on you eventually). You can quickly write down your theme and key points on separate pages and flip through them as you present.

*   Write down key phrases like "reasonable" or "primary aggressor" on flip chart pages and hang them around the room. Students can refer to these points during your topic, helping them to retain important information. You can continue adding minor points to these pages during your presentation, and connect additional terms throughout your lesson.

*   Hang blank pages on the walls when a new academy class has begun. Have the cadets write down traits they feel are important for a police officer to possess. Put the pages away until the last week of the academy, and then bring them back out. Ask your students "Have your opinions of the law enforcement profession changed?" Allow them to add to their original lists and discuss what they have learned since then.

*   Write down students responses to questions regarding your topic, but be careful not to substitute your words for the ideas they offer. You may inadvertently change the meaning offered by them causing a rift. Ask them to give you a concise description that will fit on the page.

*   When students have off-topic questions you can use the flip chart as a *"Parking Lot."* By writing their ideas down, it shows that you are interested in what they have to say. Tell the class the *"Parking Lot"* will be covered if there is enough time. If not, offer to post the answers on a police forum or other social networking website.

*   Use your flip chart as a polling station on important topics. Instead of asking for a *show* of hands (in which passive students do not participate), take the opportunity to ensure everyone is involved and out of their chairs. List the question on the flip chart, and then have each student make a checkmark indicating whether they agree or not.

*   Several of the active learning exercises in later chapters can be enhanced by using flip chart pages as part of the technique. As you read through the activities, use your imagination to determine how you might incorporate the flip chart as a resource to aid your audience in learning.

Ninja Instructor Flip Chart Skill

You do not need to be an artist to add some relevant graphics to your chart pages. One of the *Ninja instructor skills* I have learned will allow you to draw any image while talking to your audience. It sounds impossible if you are not artistic, but I assure you it is not. Find a basic image that you would like to draw to engage your class. Project the image from your computer onto the flip chart paper using a projector. Lightly trace it with a pencil so only you can see it at the front of the room. All you need to do is follow the lines with the marker during class – no thought is required for tracing pencil lines. Audiences are always compelled by the technique and connected to the presentation as they watch the creation of a relevant image.

You do not need to be an artist, but you do need to prepare ahead of time. In the illustration above, I traced the image of my police robot, giving the command to halt, onto a flip chart page. I posted the page on the wall and allowed students to list the types of conduct they thought might lead to unethical behavior. Try the technique with your next class; all it takes is a little creativity.

I have placed several images at *LEOtrainer.com/chart* for you to enhance your *Ninja skills*, but any basic image will work.

SPIM Factoid

Fear of heights is called acrophobia, fear of the dark is call achluophobia, and fear of SPIM is called logic.

Officer Neil in the year 2025

The Power of Storytelling

Your stories serve as a vital form of communication with your friends and family and a valuable method by which to train law enforcers. You can engage and educate your learners through the use of realistic, relevant, and captivating stories.

Use Stories to Enhance Understanding

Place your students in the shoes of the main character of your story – as if it is happening *here* and *now* – regardless of how long ago it was. Pull the audience in by starting out with an intriguing invitation, *"Imagine you are the one fighting the crazed man in the street, and then..."* Ask questions when you reach key decision points throughout your story, and let students feel the emotions that go along with each choice that had to be made. True stories have a *real* outcome that involved choices made by *real* people. When you make up a story that is filled with make-believe characters, it can end up in *"Never Never Land."* You may *"never"* reach your students because the made-up story *"never"* really happened to anyone – it lacks the authenticity of a real event. Audiences like relevant and interesting stories that have real people facing real conflicts and who showed character by overcoming it.

We discussed learning styles in the *Understanding Cops & Cadets* chapter. Our *Type A* extroverts are described as realistic problem solvers, and storytelling is the perfect method to train them. A funny story can be just as effective and educational as a dramatic tale. Telling stories that involve your mistakes will require some humility but they can save lives. Law enforcement is not the best profession to learn from your own mistakes, and cadets gain wisdom when you allow them to interact with your stories and characters.

> *"I am defeated, and know it, if I meet any human being from whom I find myself unable to learn anything."*
> ~George Herbert Palmer

How to Use Stories

There is nothing more powerful to have in your arsenal as a police instructor than stories. Let's say you are teaching the *Foot Patrol* topic and want students to understand what it really means to be out on foot. You could just display the SPOs on the screen and let students take notes. Let it go at that, and they will surely be ready to hit the bricks. Really, is that the best we can do for our audience? You might think, *"Well I'm teaching the day academy, I can't take them out in a dark alley to check doors at 2 a.m."* You are only partially right because you can bring that environment to the classroom. A story will allow you to take them out on foot patrol – or anywhere

> Your stories serve as a vital form of communication with others and a valuable method by which to train law enforcers.

else to experience police work.

The following story works well with the topic of *Foot Patrol*. I start with a photo of a dark alley on the screen to set the stage and then jump right into my rookie experience.

The Doorknob

It was my first night alone as a young rookie. I finished all three days of my FTO training and was fully prepared for anything that might happen [some cadets are already in shock at this point thinking they may only receive three days of training]. Jamestown was a quiet village with very little crime, and they wanted to keep it that way. One of the preventative methods we used involved checking the businesses during midnight shift to make sure no one was trying to break in or damage property.

I parked my police cruiser on the street and walked behind the businesses. It was shocking how dark it was [I turn the lights down in the room], and I was surprised at how uneasy I felt being alone. I had a gun, body armor, and plenty of training, but I was still anxious.

I had no doubt that I would get used to checking doors and maybe even catch a bad guy in the act making me an instant hero – one of many medals I would surely receive in my career.

I could hear every little noise around me and would quickly turn to see what caused them, but surely I was the only one in town who was not in bed. [I stop and draw a student in by asking a question, *"Tom, how does it feel to be in a dark alley all alone?"* Most students will not know because they have avoided dark alleys, but now – for the first time – they are really contemplating the scenario.]

The first door was the back entrance to a mom and pop restaurant where the chief routinely ate. He took me there the first day I was hired to meet the owners, and meeting them instilled in me the responsibility to protect their property. They were counting on me to get over my anxiety of the dark and check the area at night.

I approached the door with my flashlight in hand. The sergeant had previously told me that I might find an open door once a year which put me at ease. That *ease* would soon be a mistake. I grabbed the doorknob as I walked by already heading for the next business and gave it a tug. It came open and caught me completely off guard. [I stop again and pull in another student, *"Tammy, you are the one in the dark with an open door; what are you going to do?"*]

I was turning and drawing my weapon at the same time fearing someone would spring out at me. I was alone in the dark, back-peddling with a gun in my hand, and I tripped over a tree root and fell on my butt – a little pee may have even come out. [Through the use of humor, I pull in the entire class, *"Anyone else in here clumsy enough to fall on their butt?"*] I jumped up and took cover behind the tree and called for backup. I knew there was a chance I might have to fight someone or even shoot them before a deputy arrived.

An old deputy with a leather face arrived 30 minutes later to assist me. I asked him *"Do you want to go in first?"* He looked at me like I was an idiot (I would not let a nervous rookie get behind me with a gun either). He said, *"You go first, I'll be right behind you"* and he turned the doorknob. It was locked! He looked at me like I was an idiot again. All the tension and anxiety was for nothing. The doorknob was locked the entire time, but it did not latch all the way. That is, until I came along and pulled on the door. Now it was nice and secure. I served my purpose but I did not see it that way. I was embarrassed, and worse, I still had to check the rest of the doors in town.

Students need to experience the unknown that will come with a career in law enforcement. You will have no trouble pulling them into the environment using a similar story. They will connect with the feeling they experience with their *first time* of doing everything in police work – just like we did.

When you want to build tension, slow the story down and pause. Move around and do some minor acting that relates to the situation. Act like you are opening a door and give a quick look of shock as you look inside.

A five minute story can give strong insights into policing and connect students to our presentation. They can relive the experience vicariously through your story, and the connection is stronger than any other method we use. It may not fit every topic you teach – when it does – use storytelling.

"Learning without thought is labor lost." ~Confucius

Why is Storytelling so Powerful?

Have you ever been eager to share a story that you just heard during training, on the radio, or as part of a speech? Or had someone share a story with you they heard during a conference they attended?

Now, picture a class you sat through that consisted of an endless slide-after-slide presentation of bullet points. You have undoubtedly encountered this type of presentation during your academy or in-service training. Were you excited to leave the class and share bullet points of information with anyone? Do you remember anything from the presentation other than how long it was? So which type of encounter are you offering your audience?

> Were you excited to leave the class and share bullet points of information with anyone?

Lectures lack the personal connection a story can bring to your class, and stories are just as effective with veteran cops as they are with cadets. Besides engaging all three learning styles, the use of a story is a great way for extroverted students to actually learn new information.

Engage your learners by using realistic, relevant, and captivating examples. Every story you tell should help create a change in your students' thinking, behavior, attitude, emotions, or actions. And a good story will cause a change to come about much quicker than a slide filled with bullet points or a memorized SPO.

That is the power of good storytelling. It provides lasting memories of what was covered – unlike some of our other methods. It is a powerful way for you to grab your cadets' attention and provide them with relevant and lasting illustrations of police work. Storytelling is one of the most important skills you can possess as a police instructor. Add storytelling to your *Ninja instructor skills,* and reach your students like never before.

"Stories are the way we naturally think; the way we sort the natural information in our brain. They are also a way to remember – they cement ideas in our brain."
~Kate Lutz

Relevant, Relevant, Relevant

While you need to be authentic with your stories, you also need to know when to leave out information that is not relevant for the sake of brevity. If you go on with every detail for 20 minutes, the story will likely put your students to sleep. Include the details that are pertinent to your topic and leave out the rest.

You need courage to be vulnerable and personal when telling stories about situations in which you were involved. Cops are not always keen on being vulnerable in front of others, but the best storytellers have enough humility to allow themselves freedom from embarrassment.

"Your story should make a reality of law enforcement, not just describe it." ~Richipedia

A few of my best training stories are ones in which I screwed up. Fortunately, I have made it through the gauntlet, battered, but alive. Sharing your personal stories will create a connection between you and the class faster than any other method. It shows them that you are willing to be *open* with them, and that allows students to be *open* with you. It is like the safety net below the high-wire artist – without it most would not even attempt something that scary. The same can be said for your students. Many are afraid of what will happen if they open up, but when you model it for them they will feel safe enough to follow your lead.

As you tell multiple stories throughout a class, connect the important points from each one together. If they share ethical or moral choices, show their relation to one another. If you dealt with a degree of intuition show how trusting in it benefitted you or saved your life. The more you connect points together, the more knowledge they will retain.

Dramatize with Dialogue

Suppose I wanted to give a shorter illustration of *The Doorknob*. I could have said, *"I found a door open one night, but it was a false alarm."* This anecdote lacks names, specific details, and most importantly the actual dialogue that makes the original story come alive. It is still somewhat specific to the events of that night, but I doubt anyone would remember the story or the lessons attached to it.

It may not be possible for you to work dialogue into every story you tell, but you can see how the direct quotes in the original story dramatized the incident. The same will happen for your audience when you tell stories that include names, details, and quotes.

When I tell this story to law enforcement audiences, I imitate the old deputy's gruff voice *"You go first, I'll be right behind you."* It provides them with a complete picture of that night. Tell your audience the story like you would a friend, and they will relate.

Stories Create Visuals

Make it a priority to use words and illustrations that create pictures in the minds of your audience. When you sprinkle your story with images, you create a more entertaining and influential conversation for your students. The best examples are Bible stories. The Bible is filled with vivid narrations that create visuals with each line you read. Think of your favorite Bible story – the flood, the giant, the parting of the sea, or the resurrection. All bring images immediately into your mind.

Create visuals for your audience through clear and descriptive language. Do not use cloudy terms that generalize what was an exciting story. Using vigorous language will cause your story to come alive for the listener, and the small details make it memorable.

It is a good idea to ask, *"How can I put some visual detail into my story?"* Even if you are speaking without the use of slides, storytelling is visual as well as auditory. When we hear a great speaker, we can envision what they are saying without seeing a picture or video. When you hear *"Danny was standing there naked – holding a beer in his left hand and a rifle in his right,"* you have no trouble envisioning the scene in your mind. This is the interaction created by a well-told story.

How to Put Your Story Together

You want to structure your story so the audience understands the meaning behind it. The moral of the story – or key point – should become apparent during the narrative. We may ask questions during the story and discuss the implications after it is over, but it should not need a lengthy explanation. If it is confusing, you need to fix it or forget it. You should be able to smooth out problem areas with a little creativity. You do not need to include every detail as if you are writing a great work of fiction. The significant knowledge is far more important to the students than the description of some character's hair color or the way he swaggered.

Use stories that involve a conflict and a resolution. By answering the questions raised by the conflict, we teach others how to solve problems. Provide your students with real people who faced real problems. It is easy to provide our cops and cadets with the viewpoint of the officer involved, but do not forget to provide them with the viewpoint of the offender, witness, or victim as well. If you do not know exactly what their thoughts were, use that to start a class discussion. Let your students contemplate what the person was going through during the situation. Too often, we leave out the motivations of those we arrest in a story, and those are the nuggets of wisdom our cadets need.

Think about the complexity of the people in your stories and add more detail if it helps your students understand them. Take the audience on a journey so they experience the conflict of your story. Show them how it affected the officer, the suspect, and the victim. Let them experience how the characters dealt with the conflict and what lessons can be learned.

One of my family's favorite movies is *"The Princess Bride."* It has the most complex characters and conflicts you can find in one tale. You have the farm boy, *Westley,* who becomes the *Dread Pirate Roberts.* His true love, *Buttercup,* is being forced to marry a prince she does not love. Andre' the Giant plays – well, a giant – named *Fezzik.* He has a good heart but works for a bad Sicilian who kidnaps Buttercup. And my favorite, *Inigo Montoya,* is a great swordsman that has turned mercenary, but really just longs to avenge his father's murder. He has the famous line, *"Hello. My name is Inigo Montoya. You killed my father. Prepare to die."* Watch the movie if you have never seen it and see how complex the characters truly are.

I have developed a formula to ensure my stories include details and direction. You may not need to follow a format, but if you find it helpful you can use mine. Some stories may be short and only include a few of the steps while others will involve them all.

Anatomy of a Police Training Story
(Richipedia Model)

The storyteller must offer an experience that propels the listener forward through the entire story.

Set the Framework: *"You have to set the table before you can have the meal."* I have heard that advice several times from my grandfather as he would begin to tell a story; it makes more sense to me now than ever before. You cannot skip right into the conflict with no explanation of why it happened. Recreate the surroundings by setting the location (dark alley or residence), weather, and time. Include the atmosphere surrounding the events if it was relevant.

Characters Descriptions: Don't try to be *C.S. Lewis* describing the great *Aslan* in *The Chronicles of Narnia,* but take enough time to give your characters a persona. Describe their physical appearance and emotional connection to your story. Concentrate on the main characters and leave out secondary people unless they are necessary to support your message. Describe their mannerisms for the audience – were they weird, excited, quirky, or eccentric?

Consider putting the audience in the place of the main character. *"Imagine for a moment that you are the officer heading into the school. You can hear the gunshots and teenagers are running past you..."* It pulls them into the story making it their own personal experience.

The Expedition: What was the mission in your story? Why was it important? Was this a law enforcement dispatch for a crime in progress or a personal journey of faith?

The characters must encounter a challenge, conflict, hostility, opposition, or struggle to draw the interest of your audience. Some conflicts are with people and others are a personal struggle. Some may be serious, even life threatening, while others are light-hearted or funny. Try to give each person action and feeling using gestures and vocal variety.

Triumph or Defeat: This is where you provide the wisdom gained from *The Expedition.* How was the obstacle conquered? What allowed your character to persevere through their struggle? Did the main character act alone or did they have back-up of some kind? How did the encounter end? What affect was there on the characters involved and the people connected to them?

Do not be afraid to use stories involving your failures. I speak more about my failures than successes in the hopes that my students will not repeat them, and they can be more persuasive than stories with good outcomes.

The Gold Nugget: Take the knowledge gained from your story and turn it into one *gold nugget of wisdom.* Focus on one main point even if there are multiple lessons to learn. Show the class how your example can benefit them throughout their career if they choose to follow it and what could happen if they choose to ignore it.

You must decide whether you will ask questions during your story or wait until the end – it just depends on the story and how you choose to present it. Ask pointed questions that place your audience into the story. Help them to understand and feel the fear, dread, stress, intensity, achievement, and triumph of police work. You know how it feels – a story allows you to share it.

Follow-Up Investigation: See what information the students gleaned from your story aside from the main point. Ask them what created the most tension for them. The main point should connect with your topic, subject, or the SPOs. It will then support the overall lesson and add a real-life connection to the material. Make sure to wrap your stories around teaching points, and everyone will leave with the same lesson.

Which elements you choose to use will depend on *your* story and what points *you* want to make with it. I have used the following story when talking about domestic violence and the unpredictability of police work. Imagine what points you would make when using this story and what questions you would ask as a follow-up. Look for the *anatomy* of my story as you read along.

My Heroic Rescue

I was gaining confidence as a young officer in Jamestown and getting to know the *job*. It was a Sunday morning when I was dispatched for a 911 hang up. I arrived at the apartment and knocked on the door. I could hear a faint voice calling for help from inside. I banged on the door, *"Police department, open the door."* I drew my weapon and stepped back as the voice penetrated the door again, *"Help me please."* I called dispatch for back-up, but I had already decided not to wait. I kicked the door several times until it gave way and entered the room shouting commands, *"Police, let me see your hands."* I scanned the apartment for an intruder and immediately noticed a woman handcuffed to a bed. There was no one else there, but they left a trail of her clothing across the room. She tried to keep her nude body covered as I unlocked the cuffs, but it was embarrassing for both of us.

I asked her who did this to her as she caught her breath from my abrupt entry. She said, *"My boyfriend did it."* I asked her to confide in me with what had happened to her. I assured her that I would bring him to justice no matter what. She began to explain *"I wanted to surprise my boyfriend for his birthday, so I took my clothes off and then scattered them from the door to our bed. I thought he would find it sexy, so I handcuffed myself to the headboard. Then I tossed the key over by the door and waited. He was supposed to find the key when he came in last night but he never showed."* She started crying and then became angry. *"I could only reach the phone with my foot and all I could dial was 9-1-1. I'm going to kill him when he gets here!"*

I had no idea what to say, but one thing was sure, justice would be handled by her and not me. I made sure she was okay and cancelled the back-up. I was preparing myself to be compassionate for a rape victim when I first saw her handcuffed to the bed, but my plans had to adapt to the unique set of circumstances I was now faced with.

I located the woman's boyfriend and told him what happened (for his own safety). He decided to get drunk and spend the night with friends for his birthday instead of going home. *"Really bad idea,"* I explained as I shook my head. I never saw the couple again, but the officer who relieved me that night said the domestic dispute was quite astounding – I am glad I missed the encore performance.

Use Different Tactics

The first chapter of this book began right in the middle of *The Expedition* of my story, which involved a physical struggle for survival. This is a technique I like to use depending on the situation.

Begin by laying out your story using a format that works for you. Listen to the story and see where you can add moments of anticipation and climax. Consider starting your story at one of those points to build up the audience's anticipation and then stop. Go back to the very beginning and give them the background of the story. Work your way back to the climax and continue through the story until the end. This method breaks through the boredom of a lecture and gives your students a double dose of the *Triumph or Defeat*. They will be twice as likely to remember the lessons from your story this way.

> They will be twice as likely to remember the lessons from your story this way.

> *"If the story is going to have a fool, it is best for that person to be the teller of the story."* ~Thaigi

War Stories

We are dying to tell our favorite war story. It was the best of us, but if it is not relevant to the topic you have to fight the urge to use it. It will not be as good as you think if the class finds no relevance in it.

Ask yourself, *"What do I want my students to learn or experience from my story? Is this the best story to illustrate my point? Does it connect to the topic?"*

When I survey cadets, they *always* list "a good storyteller" as an attribute of their favorite instructors. The same cadets list "*irrelevant* war stories" as an attribute of their least favorite instructors. The only real difference is whether the story was relevant or not, and they know if we are telling the story to benefit them or us.

With relevance comes retention.

Most of the cadets I see after graduation greet me with a line from one of my stories. They would have been *useless* war stories had they not been relevant to the topic, but with relevance comes retention.

Collect Stories

I have a designated page in my organizer where I write down my stories; that is why *Police Instructor* is equipped with pages for *Notes, Ideas, Cases, and Stories.* When something reminds me of a story long-forgotten, and I do not write it down, it will likely be lost again. When you are reminded of a story, write down enough information so you can recall the details later. Make sure you don't lose a good story because you are too busy to write it down.

I also enjoy using other stories that are not necessarily police-related but are relevant to my topic. The following are powerful stories that I have collected and used with great success. I will give you a glimpse into each account and you can conduct your own research to use the stories effectively.

Who Was Haym Solomon? Haym was a Jewish immigrant who likely saved the United States from extinction. He was a member of the Sons of Liberty along with John and Samuel Adams, John Hancock, Patrick Henry, Paul Revere, and many other patriots who were fighting for independence. He was a wealthy entrepreneur who was arrested and sentenced to death as a spy but later escaped.

When the revolution was over, the nation was bankrupt. George Washington asked for his help and Haym delivered. Solomon gave his own fortune to the fledgling nation to keep it afloat and raised other monies as well. As a token of gratitude, then-President Washington had the Star of David added to the one dollar bill where it still is today.

Who Was Bass Reeves? Bass was born a slave in 1838. He escaped from his slave master and fled north into Indian country where he learned the skills of a warrior. In 1875, he was recruited by Judge Isaac Parker who was well known for his hangings. Bass was his most successful marshal with over 3,000 arrests. He also killed 14 fugitives during his service. When he reached the age of 68, Bass retired from marshaling and joined the Muskogee, Oklahoma Police Department (this guy makes me feel like a pansy).

Who Was Maude Collins? Maude was the first female Sheriff in the State of Ohio – back in 1925. She worked as the jail matron under her husband who was shot and killed while attempting to arrest a suspect. She took his position at the request of the county commissioners and later delivered her husband's killer to prison. She served out her husband's term and was re-elected to a second. She was famous in the area for busting up moonshine stills while her children waited in the patrol car.

Who Was Silvestre S. Herrera? Silvestre was drafted in 1944 at the age of 27 with his 4th child on the way. He grew up in Arizona; however, he was shocked to find out he was not even a U.S. citizen. The man he believed to be his father was actually his uncle. His real father was killed in a car accident and his uncle raised him as his own. His uncle told Silvestre that he was born in Mexico and therefore did not have to honor the draft notice.

Silvestre loved America and did not want anyone going to war in his place. He was part of the first American unit to land in Europe in WWII. In his first battle, he captured 8 enemy soldiers under heavy fire and saved countless American lives. During the few restful periods the soldiers had, Silvestre studied so he would be able to take his citizenship test when he made it back home.

His next battle would be devastating. His unit came under heavy fire from a machine gun nest that was protected by a mine field. Silvestre watched as dozens of his friends were gunned down. He charged through the mine field firing at the Germans, giving his comrades time to seek cover. His left leg was blown off at the knee throwing him through the air. He started firing again and advanced as another mine detonated destroying his other leg. That did not stop Silvestre Herrera. He is famous for continuing to advance with both legs amputated and pinning down the machine gun nest until the rest of the men were safe.

Silvestre survived WWII and was awarded the Congressional Medal of Honor by President Truman – all before he became an American citizen.

These and other stories like them should be heard by everyone, but they have a special place of reverence for law enforcers. They inspire us to do more than we think is possible and help us to dig deep to find our true *inner self*. These stories will provide your audience with a dynamic presentation, but only use your new storytelling powers for good.

"With great power comes great responsibility."
~Uncle Ben Parker, Spiderman

SPIM Factoid
The movie "Cujo" was the story of SPIM's lost puppy.

Designing Your Slides

This will not be a tutorial on how to build a *PowerPoint* slide show. If you need to learn the basics of the program, I have placed several tutorials on the *LEOtrainer* website; there are more available for you to watch on YouTube.

This chapter is filled with tips, illustrations, and guidelines that will help you create compelling slides that draw interest to your presentations. Strengthening your slides will help keep your audience focused and increase their retention of the material.

As the instructor, *you* are the presentation – not the slide show. If the projector fails, your laptop crashes, or you forget the jump drive, it should not matter. You should be able to go on without it. Slides should only serve as a resource to support your presentation.

Use a Simple Design

It is a good practice to pull your resources and ideas together before starting to construct a slide show. If you start with *PowerPoint,* you run the risk of building slide after slide of bullet points which is not necessarily the best design for your learners.

Humans think in narrative stories – not in bullet points. While necessary for some lists, you should try to refrain from using bullet points wherever possible, and keep the audience in mind with each slide you make.

I usually begin with my topic and a theme, but I do not work out every detail before starting to work on a new slide show. Some instructors will prefer to work out every detail before beginning; you should decide what works best for you.

Consider starting the process by using sticky notes to lay out your presentation. The technique is illustrated in the *Planning & Preparation Shortcuts* chapter.

Design Tactics

When you design your slides, look at what makes it easy for students to understand, not what is easy for you to make. If you have ever seen the show *"How It's Made"* on the Discovery channel, you can follow their lead. The show takes the confusing process of manufacturing and makes it understandable by using a narrative story with strong visuals. They go step by step until everyone understands how it is accomplished.

By using the same method that includes pictures, videos, text, and stories, you take your audience through the step-by-step process of policing. Find the clearest way possible for your students to gain the knowledge they need to be successful.

The thousands of transitions and animations available in *PowerPoint* can serve as a distraction but are enticing to use (I have fallen to their charms more than once). These elements include text that bounces, grows, flashes, dings, sings, and so on. Any elements that you add to your presentation only to benefit your amusement should be removed. Your slide show should represent who you are as an instructor. If the entire show comes across as silly, that is what your class will think of you and your credibility may suffer.

If any element is lacking relevance to the topic it should be left out. It takes discipline to decide what to include and even more to determine what to eliminate. You can break rules and take risks when you design your slides as long as you are trying to reach your students through creative means. Once again, the presentation is about them – not about how many tricks we can make *PowerPoint* perform.

Left to Right

Americans learn to read from left to right. This is a powerful principle to remember when designing a slide that contains more than one element. The area to the left of your slide should be reserved for the focus of your message – whether it is the image or the text. Your audience will look at the left side and then move to the right regardless of what is on the slide. The following introduction slide includes a photograph from the Beavercreek, Ohio Police Department.

The image of the police car serves as a relevant photo, but my title has the prominent spot on the left side of the slide where the audience's focus will initially be.

This second slide has the car on the left and the words on the right. The car will be their main focus when first viewing the slide. With such a small amount of text, students will not have much trouble looking past the car and reading the title, but with more text comes more problems.

The third slide contains far more text to the right of the image. In this type of setup, students can become distracted while trying to read past the photo. They are repeatedly drawn to look at the photo on the left as they read each line of text.

DUTIES OF OFFICER ON THE SCENE

1)Check victims & provide first aid
2)Detain witnesses & suspects
3)Conduct initial interviews
4)Preserve the scene
5)Protect & gather evidence

The fourth slide has the text in the prominent position on the left side. The students will not be distracted as they read left to right until they are finished. Try reading both and you will see the difference. Your audience will not rebel if one of your slides has a distracting arrangement, but they will quickly tire of your presentation if it is repetitive.

DUTIES OF OFFICER ON THE SCENE
1)Check victims & provide first aid
2)Detain witnesses & suspects
3)Conduct initial interviews
4)Preserve the scene
5)Protect & gather evidence

This fifth slide is the technique I use most frequently. If a photo is acting merely as an interesting supplement, and not the focus, I shrink it down and give the text prominence over the image. There is no doubt that the written information is my point of focus on this slide.

Next is a slide that I use for *Child Abduction Prevention.* During the class, kids learn how to use their bicycle to hinder a would-be abductor.

If someone grabs a child riding their bike, the kid should grab the frame; the abductor can't squeeze both into his vehicle, and they are quite hard to separate. I *could* place a large amount of text on the slide to explain the technique, but instead, I use one photo with a short title to illustrate the skill. A picture is worth a thousand words, and this one tells the story before I do. The picture, not the title, is the focus I want for my audience. It is positioned on the left side and is much larger than the text. The audience is drawn to the photo while I explain the technique in detail. A photo will greatly increase your audience's retention.

Fonts and Styles

Your typeface or font can turn into an obsession (or head ache) with hundreds to choose from. Generally, the *sans serifs* (e.g., Arial or Verdana) are better for clarity on slides. They are easier to read from a distance and look cleaner. The *serifs* (e.g., Times New Roman or Bookman Old Style) have a small projecting feature at the end of each letter. The small details help with the readability of longer publications, but they can clutter your slides.

Sans serifs offer a simple and easy-to-read appearance for slide design. If you study large signs and billboards, you will notice they are designed using sans serifs fonts. Marketers know if you cannot read the sign or billboard it is worthless, and the same is true of your presentation. Using sans serifs on your slides will make the words legible for everyone, and they will pop out on projector screens.

Take a look at the following two slides. The first is formatted using Times New Roman for the typeface. The second one uses Rockwell (also a serif) for the headline and MS Reference Sans Serif for the body. You can see how much easier it would be for your audience to read the second slide over the first – especially from a distance.

I asked cadets to vote on which sans serifs were easiest to read on a slide. They liked MS Reference Sans Serif, Arial Unicode MS, Gill Sans MT, Prima Sans BT, and Verdana. The majority of my presentations are set in MS Reference Sans Serif. I like it, the students like it, so I usually just stick with it. You can use options like bold, italics, or changes in the color of text to make it stand out.

> ### 3 OFFENSES THAT CONSTITUTE DOMESTIC VIOLENCE
>
> 1. Knowingly causing or attempting to cause physical harm to family or household members
> 2. Recklessly causing serious physical harm to a family/household member
> 3. By threat of force, knowingly cause a family member to believe that the offender will cause eminent physical harm

Serifs like Rockwell or Times New Roman are good for a change of pace, but keep them large for clarity. They work well when used for a quote or a headline (like the previous slide).

Deliver More with Text

When designing your presentation, think of the student in the back row trying to read your slides. Keep the size of text on slides 30pt. and larger whenever possible. Bigger is better when it comes to text, especially if you want your audience involved.

Most of our cops and cadets want the facts, and they want them quickly. They want to look at a simple and understandable format, and they do not want to squint. You may need to spread one SPO across four or five slides to make that happen. It is more engaging to move through four slides, spending two minutes on each one, than to show your audience a single slide that takes up eight minutes of presentation time. Use one idea per slide, and give them what they want – easily understood presentations.

Using all capital letters for a title is engaging, but they become hard to read in a sentence or paragraph. The next two slides contain the same information, but the first has all caps and the second uses lower case letters. Which one is easier to read?

OATH OF HONOR

❏AN OATH IS A SOLEMN PLEDGE
❏*HONOR* MEANS THAT ONE'S WORD IS GIVEN AS A GUARANTEE.
❏*BETRAY* IS DEFINED AS BREAKING FAITH WITH THE PUBLIC TRUST.
❏*BADGE* IS THE SYMBOL OF YOUR OFFICE.
❏*INTEGRITY* IS BEING THE SAME PERSON IN BOTH PRIVATE AND PUBLIC LIFE.

OATH OF HONOR

❏An oath is a solemn pledge
❏*Honor* means that one's word is given as a guarantee.
❏*Betray* is defined as breaking faith with the public trust.
❏*Badge* is the symbol of your office.
❏*Integrity* is being the same person in both private and public life.

Most people find it easier to read lower case text for longer passages (also known as "sentence" case). While it is easier for an audience to read lower case letters, capital letters say, *"Listen up this is important."*

Express it with Color

Choose wisely when it comes to the color of your slides. Staring at slides that use a white background can irritate your eyes, especially when you do it all day. Instead, use a dark color like black or a deep blue (my personal favorite) as your background. Your text should be white or another bright color that contrasts with the dark background.

The important point is to create a contrast regardless of your combination of colors. You can use any color combination you like, but make sure that the text jumps off the screen. If you look at a color wheel (easy to find by searching on the Internet), simply choose colors opposite from each other to create a combination that stands out.

You can make your own slide backgrounds by giving photos a dark blue or gray tint that contrasts with the white text (there are several at LEOtainer.com/backgrounds). Set the image as the new background and replace the generic *PowerPoint* choices to create a unique look for the audience. You may also choose to use a solid color for the background if the classroom is too bright. Do not be afraid to play with different background options to see what looks best.

Color will emphasize text and draw your audience's attention to an important point. The color red is assertive, powerful, bold, and emotional depending on the overall message. The color blue is considered to be dignified, professional, authoritative, loyal, and positive. Orange represents warmth, compassion, spirituality, and energy. The final color I use is yellow which is considered optimistic, fun, cheerful, happy, and inspiring. Try not to mix more than two colors of text on a single slide or it can become distracting. There are many more colors to choose from, I just stick with these few for simplicity. You will have to look up the meanings of purple, pink, or neon green for yourself.

Pictures Speak to Us

People are naturally drawn to visuals, so they should be used throughout your presentation. Using an image can double a student's recognition over the use of text alone.

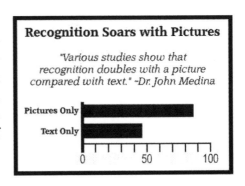

Recognition Soars with Pictures

"Various studies show that recognition doubles with a picture compared with text." -Dr. John Medina

Pictures Only

Text Only

0   50   100

The slide below is from a presentation I use for *Community Diversity*. The photo provides a powerful reference to pose a simple question and serves as a great method to start a group discussion.

The next slide shows a wreck that took the lives of four teenagers. I use this photo during *Crisis Intervention* and *Juvenile Justice* to create an impact.

As you can see, the photo makes a dramatic statement, but I left too much of the background showing. My logo on the left and a cute clipart image were distractions from the point I wanted to make. There is nothing wrong with using clipart or a logo, but they do not need to be on every slide. If they do not support the slide's message, leave them out.

I soon realized that this was a powerful picture and shrinking it down was a mistake. To make a powerful statement, consider filling the entire slide with your photo and let it stand alone. Sometimes it is best not to use any text at all and let the photo tell the story.

Remember *PowerPoint* allows you to crop pictures and move them wherever you like in the image area. In the next slide, I have taken a photo from the same tragic crash and cropped one corner of it to use as the introduction slide for *Traffic Crash Investigation.* Once again, the photo fills my slide and creates a powerful introduction for my class.

Avoid using low resolution images that will become pixilated and look crappy (a police term for unprofessional). When placing text over some images, the legibility can become a problem for your audience. Make your text easy to read by outlining the letters with a contrasting color as shown in the above slide.

There really is no reason for you not to use an image with your presentation. Finding relevant images for your topic takes very little effort. Law enforcement images are available by the thousands on the Internet, and one of the largest collections can be found at your own agency.

The Rule of Thirds

Text becomes more engaging when you place it on an angle or in a spot that is not traditional – uniquely placed text will catch a student's eye. Place it with an image on the same slide and it will create even more of an impact.

The Rule of Thirds is a principle of composition that helps you create dynamic slides. Anytime you want to *grab* the audience with a particular picture or slide, consider using this technique. I did not believe in the principle at first but now I find myself completely sold on it. Use the rule to make a powerful point.

The rule gives you eight points to work with — four lines and four intersections (shown on the previous slide). When you place items of interest along the lines, or at the intersecting points, it tends to create more visual interest and draw people in. It keeps us from plopping an image in the center of a slide where they tend to end up. On the first slide below I did just that. I stuck SPIM and his title in the center of the slide.

In the second slide, I placed him on one of the intersecting points and my title on another. The common method of placing a picture in the middle of a slide is less engaging; you can see the difference in the next few slides.

Take this picture of Cedar Falls (located in Cedarville, Ohio). The slide fails to follow *The Rule of Thirds* with the majestic waterfall centered in the photograph.

When the same waterfall is moved to one of the intersecting points, it becomes more visually appealing.

The next photo is from an *Active Shooter* training we conducted one summer at a local school. I have cropped the photo and moved the focus away from the center and placed the *Police Instructor* logo on the opposite intersecting point. It makes for a great introductory slide for the topic.

Police Instructor © 2011

The above slide depicts a police car that was originally the center of a photograph (shown below). I cropped the original image and moved the car to an intersecting point to leave room for my title, "Role of the American Peace Officer." You can see that a host of distractions are present in the original photo. The motorcycle, tool shed, dumpsters, and more cars in the background would all serve to pull interest away from the title slide. By cropping the image, and following the rule, I created a compelling image for my topic. Try the *Rule of Thirds* with some of your photos and slides to witness an appealing change.

Replace Text with Visuals

Try to replace text with pictures and images to help the audience connect with your presentation. Below is the slide I use to tell the story behind the *Graham V. Connor* ruling.

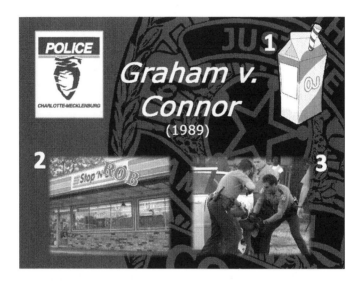

The slide contains several images that are set to appear one at a time. I begin with the Charlotte-Mecklenburg Police logo that provides the location of the incident that now determines how cops are judged when using force.

I use my remote to make the orange juice container appear on the screen and let the students wonder what O.J. has to do with their use of force requirements.

I then tell the plight of Mr. Graham who was having a diabetic attack and rushed into a store to get orange juice. I continue with Officer Connor who – because of a recent rash of robberies in the area – was sitting across from the *Stop and Rob*. I then have the image of the convenience store appear on the slide. They slowly piece the scene together through my story and images.

Graham saw a long line in the store and did not want to wait – he was about to have a diabetic attack. He rushed out to his friend's car and jumped in. They sped away to find another source of O.J. for the diabetic, but in doing so, they gave the appearance of a robbery in progress to the officer sitting across the street. Connor stopped the vehicle – Graham jumped out in a panic and was restrained when he tried to leave. Now, the picture of the officers struggling to arrest someone appears on the slide.

The images help tell the story in a memorable way that would not be possible by throwing a bunch of case law on the slide. The class will remember the ruling and the implications it has every time they use force. Ask any of my former students about Graham v. Connor, and an image of O.J. will pop into their heads followed by all the relevant details.

Next is a slide I use when teaching *Community Diversity* in the basic academy. The story is one of my favorites to tell.

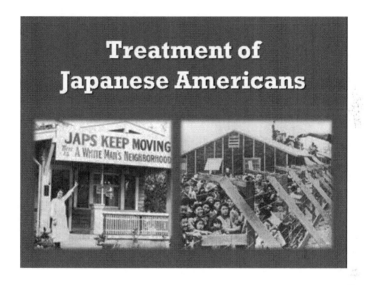

The 442nd Combat Team was filled with some incredible soldiers during WWII. The fight was much harder for them than other units because they were *Japanese Americans*. They had all been placed in the same unit because some commanders did not trust them due to their ethnic heritage. The fate of their families back home was far worse.

After Pearl Harbor, there was a great amount of anger in our nation, and rightfully so, but it was aimed at the wrong people – *Americans*. Over 110,000 *Japanese Americans*, including many of the soldier's families, were forced into War Relocation Camps and held like prisoners throughout WWII. Over 80,000 of them were *Nisei* (born and raised in America).

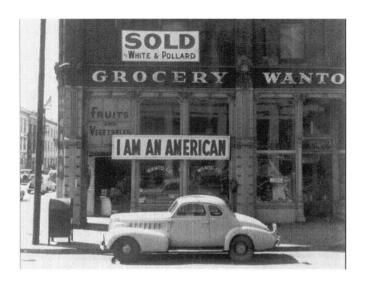

The slide above shows a store owned by a *Japanese American.* He wanted everyone to know that he was an American and also suffered when Japan attacked the U.S. The day after the photo was published in the local newspaper he was interned into a war camp and his business was closed. Talking about prejudice and racism cannot bring the reality to your audience the way pictures and stories can.

I use slides with quotes from the era, including one from the four-star general who was in charge of the camps. It helps to give the audience a feeling of just how powerful prejudice can be. By showing this picture of the general along with his quote, the students can see that real people just like them can become biased, even racist, given the right circumstances. Neither one can be an option for the guardians who serve our nation as law enforcers.

Lieutenant General John L. DeWitt,, repeatedly told newspapers that *"A JAP'S A JAP"* and testified to Congress, I don't want any of them here. They are a dangerous element.

The hatred and bias still did not stop the soldiers of the 442nd Combat Team from fighting for *their* country. They volunteered even though many of their wives and children were interned by their own nation. Would we have done the same thing? They showed unbelievable resilience and courage throughout the war and became the most highly decorated unit in American military history.

U.S. Army battle reports show the official casualty rate for the battalion, combining KIA (killed in action) with MIA (missing in action) and WIA (wounded in action), was over 93%.

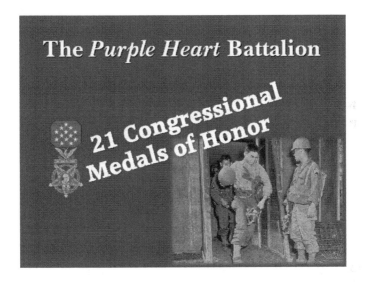

This slide points out their achievement of 21 Congressional Medals of Honor, but I proudly finish listing their other awards myself. That keeps me as the source of important information instead of my slide show, and I am proud to have worn the same uniform as they did.

The soldiers also received:

* ✯ 9,486 Purple Hearts for only 3,000 soldiers (you do the math)
* ✯ 7 Presidential Unit Citations (5 earned in one month)
* ✯ 52 Distinguished Service Crosses
* ✯ 560 Silver Stars with 28 second awards
* ✯ 22 Legion of Merits
* ✯ 15 Soldier's Medals
* ✯ 4,000 Bronze Stars with 1,200 second awards

That is an impressive list that hopefully will never need to be repeated. The 442nd accomplished all that while much of our nation discriminated against them and their families. They deserve to be honored by passing on their story to others who will encounter racism and bias on a daily basis.

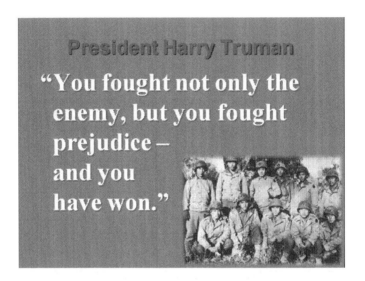

Replacing the text with images can change the entire feel of your presentation – especially your stories. Imagine the story of the 442nd Combat Team without the photographs. It might still stir your audience but not as much as when they see the faces of those who were forced behind barbed wire because of their heritage.

Keep Text Short

Simplicity is a key principle of good slide design – clutter is hard to read. The following slides contain text describing the Supreme Court's ruling on Graham v. Connor. The first looks more like notes than a supporting slide for a presentation. The second slide states the main point, *"Reasonable officer facing a rapidly-evolving situation,"* from the decision. The rest of the information should come from the presenter, and more details can be provided through handouts if necessary. The slide also includes an image of O.J. that serves as a memory tool. It grabs the attention of the students and it reminds me of what to say as well.

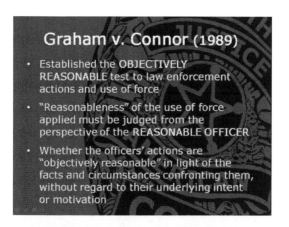

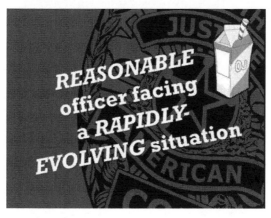

People cannot read long sentences and listen to you at the same time. Your slides should contain brief statements that can be easily read before you begin talking. They should also serve as key points that will remind you of what needs covered.

Videos Provide Clarity

Unlike when I was in the academy, a multitude of sources to obtain police-related videos are now available. You can give your students realism without making them leave their seats.

Video is not only a welcome change for cops and cadets but a powerful way to prove an important point. When you have a long topic to cover, it is even more important to change up and follow

The 10 Minute Rule by adding videos. You cannot tell a class over and over *"this is how it is done"* and expect them to understand what *"this"* is without real-life examples. A relevant video will support your message and eliminate possible confusion caused by other methods.

I have built my collection of law enforcement videos over time, but some of them do not involve policing. They can still be effective learning tools for your audience as long as they are relevant. Visit *LEOtrainer.com/videos* for a moment, and watch the scene from *What Happens in Vegas*. I use the clip to instruct the assault statute. It is not only funny, but it helps my audience clearly understand the elements of assault. Every video you use does not have to involve law enforcement, but they should reinforce your point in a meaningful way.

Try to keep most of the videos you use under three minutes, otherwise they can take over your presentation. The videos are only a tool we use to make a point. I collect clips from TV shows like *A&E's Rookies* (see next slide), *Border Wars, Street Patrol, Alaska State Troopers, Cops, Crime 360, Police P.O.V.,* TLC's *Police Women,* and others. Channels like *A&E, TLC, The Discovery Channel, TruTV,* and *National Geographic* routinely have marathons of their reality shows making your job easier. With the right software, you can use these shows, your DVDs, and YouTube clips to create a large collection of training videos in a few days.

Using Your Videos

There are several brands of software available that will pull videos from DVDs and the Internet. You can then edit them in your computer and embed the videos directly into your slide show. If you convert them into Windows Media Video (WMV) files, they are easy to use with *PowerPoint*. I have tried several brands of software over the years, but *Wondershare* offers the best capabilities for your money. I find it to be the best all-around program to download and edit your videos (a direct link to the program can be found at *LEOtrainer.com/videos*.)

Your audience will appreciate your efforts to trim a video down to the relevant two minute scene instead of playing an entire episode that has little or no relevance. Once you embed a video into your slide show, there is no need to stop the presentation and switch over to a DVD/VHS player or pull up the Internet to play the clip. When you click the remote and advance to the next slide, your video will automatically play. It provides for a seamless transition for your audience and removes unnecessary distractions.

Marking the previous slide with a small star in the bottom right hand corner is a good method to remind you of the coming video that you need to introduce.

You can also take a video from YouTube, remove the sound, and narrate the video while it plays for your class. It keeps you in command of your presentation and the audience will focus on you – not just the video.

Too much Data is a Distraction

When you use too many types of data – charts, graphs, and statistics – it can confuse the most seasoned audience. Graphs and charts are easy to make with *PowerPoint* but not always easy to understand. If it looks confusing to you, it surely will be confusing to your students. If the data distracts from the information, get rid of it or figure out a way to simplify it. Make the data large to give it impact, and then add an image to enhance it.

Ask yourself three questions when using data:
1. What point am I trying to make?
2. How will using it support my message?

3. Is there an easier way to communicate my point without using graphs or charts?

If the data is essential, make it stand out from the rest of your information. For instance, if you are teaching the *Domestic Violence* topic, you may want to use the study of officers killed in the line of duty.

Your point will stand out by highlighting the slice of the chart in red that shows how many officers were killed while on domestic violence calls (32%). Place the remainder of the pie chart in a grey tone for a strong contrast. After the class views your slide, it will be hard for them not to remember the risks involved when they respond to a domestic violence call, and the number will likely stick in their memories forever.

Handouts Not Slides

Handouts, if given, should complement your slides, not replicate them. Your slides should not be detailed enough to work as a handout by themselves. Slides should assist you as a tool; they should not be used as notes – for you or for your students. Using handouts that contain blanks engage the cadets in their learning as they fill the information in.

This next image is a handout I use for the Ohio Revised Code section covering *Homicide*. The slide that follows the handout is what the cadets see on the screen.

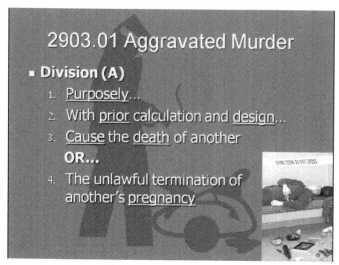

I fade in each line, one by one, and give my cadets time to fill in the blanks. I then take a few minutes to discuss what each word means as part of the elements of the crime. This technique provides for various learning styles and allows students to leave with information in their heads and hands.

Use an Introduction Slide

Start out with a simple slide introducing you, your topic, and a relevant image. That's it. Relegate the slides and graphics to a supporting role; what you say, and how you say it, is of greater importance than what is on your slide.

Officer Richard Neil

Legal 2-2C

Sexual Assault

Tell–Then Show

A good strategy is to *tell them, and then show them.* Some trainers will advance to the next slide, use it as their notes, and then begin to tell the audience what it is about. The *Tell–Then Show* method might take more effort, but it sends a better message.

Start talking about your next point while on the previous slide. After a few seconds, advance to the next slide that displays the information you are currently talking about, and the class will see you are in command of the presentation. They realize that the important material is based on your experience as a cop, and the presentation is not just a script you are reading from. Even if you only use this method two or three times throughout the presentation, it will build credibility with your students – especially when training skeptical veteran officers.

I developed this method over a decade ago to break myself from the bad habit of reading the slides to my class. It takes a long time to develop bad habits, so do not expect to break them overnight. Start making changes today.

Use Pauses

Pause for a moment when you introduce a new slide; think about what you are talking about and give your audience a moment to absorb the new information. Students will want to read the text, look at the images, and listen to you. Since they cannot do all three at once, something will be ignored – most likely you. Give them a moment to look at the information and shift their attention back to you before speaking.

Add Drama with a Blank Screen

You do not need to have a slide showing all the time. Many remotes offer a button allowing you to blank the screen. You can also hit the "B" key on your keyboard to cause the screen to go blank during any *PowerPoint* show. This helps the students to focus their attention back on you and not on the current slide. This is a very effective technique to use when making key points during a presentation. If someone asks a question, blanking the screen can help the audience focus on the discussion instead of splitting their concentration with the image on the screen.

The Agenda Slide

With long topics, consider pulling up an agenda slide from time to time as a reminder of where you have been and where you are going. It can be helpful for topics that are spread across several days to give students this quick refresher before moving on. I use the slide below during *Search & Seizure* to keep my students on track – pointing out where we are, where we have been, and where we are going.

Another great way to keep students on track is to use a flip chart. Write your theme and the key points of your presentation on the pad as you progress throughout the day. It will stand next to the screen as a constant reminder of what has been covered.

Search & Seizure
At a Glance
- Reasonable Suspicion
- Probable Cause
- Exclusionary Rule
- Plain View
- Exigent Circumstance

Copyright for Police Instructors

Copyright can be confusing and misunderstood by police instructors. Many of our instructors believe it is illegal to use videos, photos, and images that are the property of another. This is true unless you are involved in the education field – which you are as an academy instructor, in-service trainer, or criminal justice educator. If you follow the established rules, you can use all the different types of media previously listed.

Fair use *explicitly* allows use of copyrighted materials for educational purposes such as teaching, criticism, comment, news reporting, scholarship, and research. Rather than listing exact limits of fair use, the copyright law provides four standards for determination of the exemption (which are available at LEOtrainer.com/copyright).

An important thing to consider when deciding if you are violating copyright is the effect on marketability. If there will be no reduction in the sales because of copying or distributing the work, the fair use exemption is likely to apply. If your use as a police instructor will cause a decrease in sales for the copyright holder, it is a violation. You should not be copying videos and handing them out as a trainer. You should be using them to help your learners understand new concepts. If you follow the rules, you should never damage the copyright holder's ability to make money from their product.

When I purchased the DVD of *A&E's Rookies* and then used *Wondershare* to edit out a two-minute segment, I did not hurt their future DVD sales by playing that clip for cadets. If anything, they may want to go out and buy it for themselves. But, if I take that clip and several others from the DVD and make copies for all of my instructor friends, I could easily be accused of decreasing sales. The other instructors would no longer feel the need to purchase the DVD for themselves.

If you have questions about usage rights, always consult your academy commander, law director, or appropriate supervisor. More information is available at copyright.gov.

Review-Make Corrections-Improve

Always proofread your work; then proofread it again. Take the time to look for typos and errors. One mistake is not a big deal, but repeated errors throughout your presentation look unprofessional and become a distraction.

After I make a *PowerPoint* presentation, I always find elements – and at times entire slides – that can be removed. It is not always easy to remove something you just created, but you should look at what is best for your audience. It is a good practice to review your slide show after creating it, but take a break first and clear your head. Each time I instruct a topic I review my accompanying slide show. It reminds me of what I am going to say and when I will be saying it. I continually look for information that needs updated or can be improved upon.

Every *PowerPoint* presentation you design should incorporate large and legible text, images, and several videos that relate to the topic. I have included dozens of *PowerPoint* presentations at *LEOtrainer.com/slideshows* to help you get started. Download them and play with the features to see what you like – it's the best way to learn.

> *"So be sure when you step, Step with care and great tact. And remember that life's A Great Balancing Act. And will you succeed? Yes! You will, indeed! (98 and ¾ percent guaranteed)"* ~Dr. Seuss

Some Rules are Made to be Broken

Trust in your own creativity, and don't be afraid to break the rules if the situation calls for it. While these tips have worked well for me, at the end of the day they are my preferences. Feel free to use them, ignore them, or create your own methods of design. Use common sense and good judgment when you lay out your slides, and the audience will benefit from your efforts.

As a famous Jedi once told me: *"Do or do not – there is no try."* ~Yoda

SPIM Factoid

SPIM was Yoda's first padawan. He was sent to our galaxy after he overshadowed the Force.

Increasing Audience Participation

*"If you've got them by the balls, their hearts
and minds will follow." ~John Wayne*

When you instruct, you are responsible for passing along wisdom – not just information. Engaged cops and cadets are enthusiastic to learn and become active participants in their own training. To create productive, memorable, and vibrant classes, an instructor must continually work on increasing audience participation. A good format will include group discussions, lectures, guest speakers, case studies, review games, and other activities. Active learning and audience participation may require more from you as an instructor but, the payoff for the audience is worth it. Your efforts will benefit them with a deep understanding of the topic and prepare them for the tasks that lay ahead.

It is difficult for cadets to comprehend the serious nature of law enforcement if they sit and listen to lecture after lecture without any real examples. I admitted to my near-death blunder at the beginning of this book – as I do to my classes – because there are lessons to be learned. While the responsibility to survive falls on the officer in *that moment,* we share in that responsibility as their instructor. If we fail to gain the participation of our audience, we may send them into the field as unprepared as I was.

"There is only one way under high heaven to get anybody to do anything. Just one way. And that is by making the other person want to do it." ~Dale Carnegie

The Academy is Crucial

I feel ill every time I hear a cop tell a new rookie, *"Forget everything you learned in the academy,"* or *"A month in the academy isn't worth one hour on the street,"* or the worst, *"The academy is over – now you'll learn how to be a real cop."*

The academy is crucial to the success of our cadets and this type of careless statement can cause confusion. Every topic has real-world implications if the instructor puts forth the effort to make it *real.* Even if you do not like the curriculum, there is always important information you can add. Your personal knowledge and experience is the most valuable teaching resource you have, and those nuggets are what your students need the most, and what they look forward to.

> Every topic has real-world implications if the instructor puts forth the effort to make it *real.*

Experiential Activities

Our audience of law enforcers and cadets learns best by *doing,* and any activity that provides them with a direct experience will help them understand more effectively.

"For the things we have to learn before we can do them, we learn by doing them." ~Aristotle

You can design your own experiential activities or adapt those created by others to gain the participation of your audience. These activities can add relevance and understanding where a lecture and bullet points cannot. I created *Neil Island* with the help of my daughter, Nadia. I originally created the exercise to force students to take a deep look at the components of our criminal justice system, but it works well with other topics including *Community Policing, Community Diversity, Crime Prevention, Crisis Intervention, and others.*

Neil Island

Break your class into small groups, and provide them with copies of the following story (or display it on the screen).

You have joined others in starting a new society on Neil Island, but even with a careful selection process, crime has become an issue. There is a prison, but it only has room for five people. They will each have their own cell, but they must share the common areas like bathrooms and the recreation facilities. There is no separation available, and no system of parole or probation exists due to financial cuts.

Queen Nadia (she wanted to be queen of Ohio, but I gave her an island instead) has issued a proclamation to deal with this scourge on society by setting an example. Your citizens will decide the fate of the following people who have been convicted. The prisoners include:

1. A 50-year-old man who hired a hit-man to kill his son-in-law. The victim was physically abusing the suspect's daughter for years.

2. A 27-year-old single mother of two convicted of a DUI accident that killed a 38-year-old man. He was a devoted husband and the father of three kids.

3. A 16-year-old burglar who was caught stealing an XBox from a neighbor's house. He cooperated and confessed to three other burglaries in the area.

4. A 37-year-old man who abducted and repeatedly raped a 5-year-old girl. She was rescued after 10 days of captivity.

5. An 18-year-old gang member who was a passenger in a car that was involved in an armed robbery. A pursuit of the

vehicle resulted in a crash that killed a police officer. She left a husband and her 6-month-old infant behind.

6. A 41-year-old man arrested while driving a stolen car. The car belongs to a missing woman who has never been found. The man has a previous conviction for rape.

7. A 26-year-old male teacher who had a *consensual* relationship with a 15-year-old student. The student said he loved his teacher and admitted that they were sexually involved.

8. A 13-year-old male who was caught molesting his two female cousins, ages 3 and 6. He has no criminal record but the victims' parents want him locked away forever.

The citizens must follow the sentencing options based on the Queen Nadia's proclamation, the available space, and the budget set for confinement.

1. One person *must* be executed. Try to make this a unanimous decision among your group.

2. One person *must* receive life in prison without parole.

3. One person *must* receive 20 years in prison.

4. One person *must* receive five years in prison.

5. One person *must* receive three years in prison.

6. One person *must* receive six months in prison.

7. Two people *must* go free with no punishment or court controls of any type.

Give the teams 20 to 45 minutes to work on their list (depending on the size of your groups). Some groups will want the option to give up. Force them to choose a sentence for each person. As officers, they will not have the option to give up. They need to experience the reality that some decisions in their career will be difficult to make. No one will want the responsibility of making them – they must make them just the same.

Each group must indicate who they executed and why. They must explain what influenced their decisions on who received the harshest sentence compared to the lightest. Have each group present their choices to the class and then compare the differences.

Did they lock up the 13-year-old? Will he simply become a better predator from the experience with other sex offenders all around him? Was he a victim himself? Most groups choose to execute the 37-year-old child abductor instead of the man who committed a premeditated murder even though capital punishment is not an option for such a crime in the real world. Ask them how they can rationalize such a decision? There are dozens of questions you can ask based on their discussions.

Ask how many members in a group had a difference of opinion. Go through the list one by one discussing the good and bad reasons for execution, imprisonment, or giving that particular person another chance. Talk about the ethics of our legal system as well as its inherent flaws.

Begin a class discussion by asking, *"Do we really need services like probation, parole, child protective services, psychiatric hospitals, and rehabilitation centers?"* Encourage an in-depth discussion on the importance of social services and incarceration, including the improvements that are needed in our current system. Ask them *"What was the most frustrating part of the activity for you?"*

This is one of the most compelling experiential activities that I have created. Deep discussions and strong arguments will occur. Be a facilitator and let the students control their group discussions. Stay out of their way unless they are getting completely off-track. Walk around and listen to their discussions, and take your own notes to use for the end of the exercise. The students will look at the different services in a new light when they are burdened with the responsibility to make decisions that will affect the community, the victim, the suspect, and both of their families.

Neil Island is thought-provoking and involves emotional situations that create a challenging activity for students, so make sure you have enough time before using this experiential activity. This activity can last 45 to 90 minutes depending on your class size and the depth of their discussions.

There are several more experiential activities for you to use in the *Active Learning Index,* and consider developing your own from cases that have challenged you.

Benefits Not Features

Visit a car lot tomorrow and you will deal with someone who specializes in selling you more car than you need. They can convince the average buyer to purchase the prettier, bigger, and bolder car. Why is that? One of the secrets of a salesman is to point continually to the benefits instead of the features. The principle is referred to as *"features tell, benefits sell."*

Would it draw you in if a salesman spent all his time talking about the air bags? A more experienced salesman will point to the thousands you will save on fuel with 40mpg. He will speak of the all-wheel drive system that will whisk you through the snow this winter, the heated mirrors that will keep you from getting out in the cold, and the ultra comfortable interior that fits you like a glove. Those are the items that help you see, and feel, the benefits.

Officers also follow the principle of *benefits* when conducting an interrogation. *"You should not lie to the police,"* is a feature often used unconvincingly. However, a smart officer will provide the benefits of confessing, *"A weight will be lifted off of you by telling me the truth"* or *"I will tell the prosecutor you cooperated, and he may cut you a break"* or for Andy Sipowicz, *"I won't need to use the phone book on you again."* The more benefits shown, the quicker they talk.

What seems to be an obvious benefit to you as a veteran of policing may completely elude your students. Make sure to always reinforce the features of your lesson, but highlight the benefits to increase audience participation.

Debate is a Powerful Learning Tool

The *Type A* extroverts in our audience like to be involved in the learning process and always enjoy a good debate. A well organized debate will allow students to see past their personal bias and look at the information from multiple points of view.

For a debate: Create two debate teams and a press corps. Provide the teams with ample time to develop a strategy and create examples to support their position. The students in the press corps will work as journalists and ask questions of both sides. They will spend the preparation time thinking of challenging questions that the media might ask an officer about the issue.

Let each team give a short opening argument and then allow the other team to rebut. After each team has a chance to speak, have one of the students from the press corps ask a question of each group. Only one person from each team should speak at a time with the remaining members acting as their advisors. Instruct the teams to select a different student to speak for each round. This keeps everyone involved and does not allow for anyone to zone out or take over.

Ethics is the topic in the following example. The debate is based on a book passage, but any relevant resource will work. In *Unleashing the Power of Unconditional Respect,* Jack L. Colwell and Charles Huth speak about law enforcement's need for personal *anima* or true inner self. They offer the following realizations for law enforcers to build upon.

* I am a human being endowed with the gift of self-examination. In other words, I have a conscience, and I am therefore responsible for my thoughts, words, actions, and inactions.

* I am *not* a simple stimulus-response mechanism. I cannot simply blame others for my reactions and responses.

* I must face the fact that I have prejudices, loyalties, desires, and fears that cloud my judgment and shroud me in self-deception. When I am wrong, I will almost certainly deceive myself with self-justification and direct blame at other people and circumstances – I will naturally assume that I am right at my most wrong points.

Is the above *anima* desperately needed in law enforcement as the authors claim? Can showing unconditional respect to everyone you encounter as a law enforcer benefit you physically, psychologically, and even tactically as they suggest in their book?

You can use resources like the Rodney King video or the case of Clarence Elkins from Ohio to fuel the debate.

Team 1 will represent the law enforcers who deal with suspects that spit on them, assault them, and kill them just for being an officer. They will point out the fault with trying to show respect to such foul people in our society and argue that showing respect to a criminal makes an officer appear weak. How might showing unconditional respect hurt them, their families, and society as whole?

Team 2 will represent the members of the community. They will point out the sworn duty of each officer to respect all citizens. They will argue from the viewpoint of someone who has been rehabilitated and should not be shown disrespect because of their past choices. They will also argue as the family members of the person who has paid their debt to society or has been wrongfully accused.

Press Corps members will ask questions of both sides. They will act as the devil's advocate and engage each team with challenging questions regarding the issue of respect. Encourage them to keep a neutral view of the topic and pose relevant, as well as controversial, questions.

Do not allow your students to pick the side they represent during the debate. Bring the topic up during your presentation and ask for a show of hands to indicate which viewpoint each audience member holds. Take the students who were passionately in favor of one viewpoint and assign them to the team that will oppose it.

This debate illustrates the challenges students will face when they are asked to protect and serve people they don't like; and they will learn the value of understanding both sides of a situation.

You can create a debate activity for *every* topic you teach. Let's be honest; if there were only two cops on your department, they would find something to argue about. That is why this learning method is so effective.

The *15 & Criminal* activity located in the *Active Learning Index* is another debate exercise that I use for *Juvenile Justice*, but other activities throughout *Police Instructor* can be easily adapted as well – use your imagination.

> Let's be honest; if there were only two cops on your department, they would find something to argue about.

Draw a Card, Any Card

Whenever you want to increase participation, pull out a deck of cards. Have each student write their name on one playing card and mix it back into the deck (you can also use index cards). I use a deck of *magic* cards that are blank on one side (a common item in dollar stores).

Have your students take turns drawing a card to choose who will answer the next question, take part in a role-play, or be chosen to get you fresh coffee. Your learners will enjoy the change of pace, and there are several benefits gained from using this simple technique. It helps you to learn the names of your audience, eliminates only calling on those students who always have their hands up, and forces everyone to pay closer attention to your presentation knowing that they may be chosen next.

You can add more interest to the technique by adding consequences. Let a different student pick a card each time. If their chosen classmate answers correctly, give both of them praise or prizes (they prefer candy). But if their classmate answers incorrectly, they both have to pay the price (a few pushups, sit-ups, or they lose the candy they have already won). Let your class decide on the *penalty* for a wrong answer – it is more fun that way. If they've had physical training all day, I provide them with another option. They can choose to stand up and announce to the class, *"I want to be like Officer Neil when I grow up,"* instead (yes, I love my work). They usually just do the push-ups.

The students who normally go with the safe response of *"I don't know,"* will now pay attention to your presentation because there is more at stake. They not only hold their own fate in their hands but that of a classmate as well. This helps to reinforce that their actions, decisions, and preparations will affect the lives of other officers and citizens as well.

After a student's card is selected, never put it on the bottom of the deck. Make sure everyone is watching as you shuffle it back in with the rest. They are not *home free,* and can be called upon again at any time – it's the luck of the draw.

Cadets thrive under the pressure of being called upon without warning and gain confidence when they are put on the spot and answer a question correctly. If they get it wrong, they know what they need to work on.

Interactive Methods Show Comprehension

You want your students to be able to show you their ability to employ what you have taught them. This concept should not be confined to firearms, driving, and defensive tactics. You can design interactive methods that will benefit your students when they encounter a real situation regardless of the topic. This goes beyond passing a written test.

In a real call involving a shoplifter, a cadet will not receive four multiple choice answers from which to choose. Students need to show their ability to make a decision based on a situation – not on possible test answers. Decisive action and logical thinking will be required of them in law enforcement, and we should prepare them by requiring hard decisions to be made in the academy.

Put them in the position of a decision maker as often as you can. It does not matter how complex or simple, how stressful or calm, or how important or petty the decision may be. Your students will need an arsenal of decision-making skills. Each time they make a choice under your instruction, they will become more confident in their ability to make a decision on the street. Consider the following example to coax tough decisions from your cadets:

Macaroni and Cheese

You are dispatched on a shoplifting call to a local grocery store. When you arrive, the manager has a woman in the front office and demands charges be filed against her for theft – a routine call for any agency. The woman is crying and says she has three kids counting on her. *What would you do?* [Have each student write their answer on an index card and turn it over. Once everyone has written an answer pick a few to look at and discuss the answers with the class.]

You handcuff her and take her to your patrol car. You walk over to her vehicle to conduct a search and see three children inside. They are sleeping amongst clothes, toys, and empty food packages. *What would you do? Is this woman a bad mother?* [Use the index cards again to ensure everyone is making a decision. Consider having the students trade their card with someone else and having that person read off the answer, and discuss the choice that was made.]

You go back to your cruiser and question the woman. She explains that they are homeless and living out of her car. Her husband left them and took everything. She was stealing *Macaroni and Cheese* to feed her kids and admits she has done it several times in the past few weeks. *What would you do?*

When you search the vehicle, you find dozens of job applications and a date book filled with appointments for job interviews. The three children are healthy and obviously love their mother, but you are there on a theft investigation. *What would you do?* [Once again, start with the index card to make sure everyone answers the next complex question. This is a great discussion starter.] *If you were in the same situation as the woman and had no other way to feed your kids, would you steal the food?*

This is a good scenario to use with *Ethics, Crisis Intervention,* or other relevant topics. Do not tell your audience the entire story at once. Stop at the strategic points and pose the questions to your students letting them think the situation through. It is easy to say every *thief* should go to jail until you run into a situation like this one.

I was challenged as a young officer when I responded on this call. I had my own children, and I was perplexed when I thought about what I would be willing to do if I found myself in the same situation as the woman. I did not arrest the mother of three that day. I paid the manager for the food she had stolen, and my shift chipped in and bought more groceries for the family.

Did we do the right thing? I don't know, but it is a great question to pose to your class. Use complex situations that you have been involved in to create interactive lessons for your audience, and they will gain wisdom by sharing your experience.

Role-Playing and Scenario Based Learning

Role-playing and scenario-based learning can be used in the same manner as a virtual reality simulator. By taking on the role of a cop at a domestic violence call, cadets are interacting with the material instead of just taking notes on it. While some students participate in the role play, the others can watch, listen, and later review with them. Their memory will be enhanced from these exercises because of the interaction with other cadets, and a new understanding of the information will emerge.

Role-playing requires preparation on the part of the instructor before it starts. You should have a clear understanding of what skills you want the cadets to learn through the scenario you choose. If you are using role-play as part of the *Domestic Violence* topic, you will not need to make up a scenario. It is easier to give your students an actual police report to study as a script, and have them loosely follow it. Use cadets to fill every role in your scenario: the fighting couple, their children, the bystanders, and the responding officers. Let them see the situation from every possible viewpoint and consider the emotional state of each person involved. The following is a short example of a role-play I have used with great results.

You respond to a request for assistance by the paramedics. They are treating a woman with a head injury under suspicious circumstances, and they are concerned for her safety.

You arrive at a middle class home to find a woman complaining of head pain. She is home alone and states that her husband is at work. You see bruising on the right side of her face including her eye, ear, and jaw area. She winces and grimaces in pain when moving around. Breathing appears to be painful, and she is holding her side. [Cadets begin to react to the situation]

The woman says she was struck by the refrigerator door while cleaning earlier. She also complains of pain around the left side of her face that increases when she opens and closes her jaw. She denies any other injuries and is reluctant to answer questions about her wounds or her husband. She wishes to be transported to the emergency room and says, *"Please stop asking me all these questions I just want to go to the hospital."* [Cadets learn to deal with an uncooperative victim and must conduct a follow-up investigation with the husband]

When the role-play is over, make sure to debrief *all* the cadets together. Start by asking them what went well and what did not. Their answers will let you know if it was successful as a learning tool or if they were confused with your presentation. Spend time going over what you observed during the exercise and point out what was done well and what needs improvement.

I have had success using students from *theatre class* to act as the role players allowing the cadets to focus on the training, but that may not always be an option. Role-play exercises have great training value, and when done right by the instructor, will greatly enhance any students learning experience. The success of the activity will depend on how well you prepare the students and the material.

Cops & Robbers & Judges

Cops & Robbers & Judges is a role-play method that requires your cadets to see a situation from several different perspectives. The students take turns playing police officers, perpetrators, and judges. You will merely be a facilitator for the exercise.

Begin by providing the class with a basic understanding of your topic through a lecture or demonstration of the proper tactics for the situation. After your initial training, have the students practice the skills as a team and continually work to improve their technique.

For this example, you are conducting a class on *Stops & Approaches*. After explaining and demonstrating the basics of a traffic stop to your class, you will need to develop their abilities to actually conduct a stop. You can accomplish this by presenting them with different scenarios. At first, have two students play the cops, one play the robber, and three act as the judges.

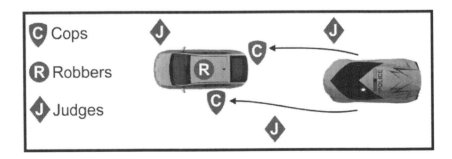

The Cops will initiate and conduct a traffic stop using the information you provided prior to the activity. The Robber should be given a basic scenario to follow, and provide your Judges with a checklist to observe and evaluate the Cops' performance.

The Judges will concentrate on evaluating the scenario and not interact with the Cops or Robbers until the exercise is completed. Once finished, they can discuss which skills were performed well and which need improvement. The students will rotate their responsibilities and the new Cops will conduct the next traffic stop. Make sure they can perform their new skills correctly before you finish the activity. Repetition is a key component to learning any new skill effectively.

Stops & Approaches Checklist

☐ Was the officer ready to exit their patrol unit as soon as the suspect vehicle came to a stop?

☐ Did the officer check for traffic before exiting?

☐ Did the officer make sure the trunk was secure?

☐ Did the officer check for anyone hiding in the back seat or floorboard of the suspect's vehicle?

☐ Did the officer keep their distance from the suspects grasp? Did they use a strong bladed stance?

☐ Did the officer keep their weapon hand free?

☐ Did the officer ensure the suspect's hands were visible at all times? Passenger's hands?

☐ Did the officer secure the drivers license so they were not encumbered by it?

☐ Did the officer follow safe procedures for arrest and search of the perpetrator and their vehicle?

Cops:
Robbers: Judge:
Notes:

Instead of only involving one student with the exercise (while the others sit around waiting their turn), you will have everyone involved in the learning process. They will see the activity from several different points of view, and when they act as Judges, the students are constantly watching for mistakes; and it helps them recognize their own.

You may want to follow the initial activity with a more intensive battery of scenarios; this method will help your students build a strong foundation to prepare. Cops & Robbers & Judges will also work with other training exercises like: *Prisoner Booking & Handling, Domestic Violence,* and *Building Searches.*

Props Engage the Audience

"I watched a couple of really bad directors work, and I saw how they completely botched it up and missed the visual opportunities of the scene when we had put things in front of them as opportunities. Set pieces, props and so on." ~James Cameron

The master creator of *Avatar* and *Titanic,* James Cameron, teaches the value of props. You are the director of your presentation; don't miss visual opportunities by not using an available prop. Using a relevant item with your topic can grab the attention of your audience, and just knowing you took the time to bring something in shows students that you are interested in being an exceptional instructor. You have taken a step that many instructors will not, and the class will be engaged just wondering why you brought the item with you.

Topic areas like *Evidence Collection Techniques* become more effective with the use of props. You can bring in a fingerprint kit with brushes, powder, and tape, so students can dust for latent prints. These are important skills that lecturing alone can never teach.

I take the class outside to my personal vehicle and have them dust it for prints. To make it easy for them, I let them stick a handprint where they know to find it. They enjoy getting my Jeep dirty and it shows them that I am making a personal investment (the reality is I only wash it once a year anyways).

It helps them to build confidence when they start out easy, but that is not the real world. We must continue to challenge them further. Next, I encourage students to check their own vehicles for evidence, but this time only for latent prints. They must use a little thought to determine where they commonly touch their vehicle and where a thief would touch it as well. They struggle to find latent prints at times disappointing their *CSI*

Miami expectations. They begin to understand the difference between the real world of law enforcement and *Hollywood's* portrayals.

> They begin to understand the difference between the real world of law enforcement and Hollywood's portrayals.

I finish the lesson by having them pick out garbage from the trash cans. Pop cans, potato chip bags, coffee cups, and bottles are items commonly found. Students must continue to process the garbage until they find, and lift, three identifiable prints. They learn that great looking prints are not found everywhere they look, but through determination, they can locate valuable evidence. All of the items are props – including the trash – that help my students learn a new skill.

Outside of their training in the academy, some officers will never receive any other formal instruction on your topic. It is up to you as their instructor to equip them with what they need.

Some other less obvious topics that work well with props include *Missing Children Investigation* and *Missing Persons*. Search and Rescue expert Robert J. Koester developed the handbook *"Lost Person Behavior"* to serve as a guide to search for the lost. *The National Center for Missing and Exploited Children* worked with Mr. Koester to develop information for lost and abducted children. This provides law enforcement and rescue personnel with a starting point to begin our search. It is a straightforward method that you can teach to any audience, but you will need a few props to be effective.

You will need a map that includes the location of your class and a protractor (or pencil and string). Separate your class into small groups and provide each team with a map and the following statistics. The research tells us that when a 3-year-old is lost in an urban environment they are found within .1 miles from the spot they were last seen 25% of the time. Have the groups draw a circle around the reported missing location on their map representing the 25% probability of .1 miles. Have them continue drawing circles for each area of probability as follows: .3 miles 50%, .5 miles 75%, and .7 miles 95%.

The following slide is a map laid out using the percentages for a lost 3-year-old. The image will provide your groups with an example of how to layout their maps before they start the exercise.

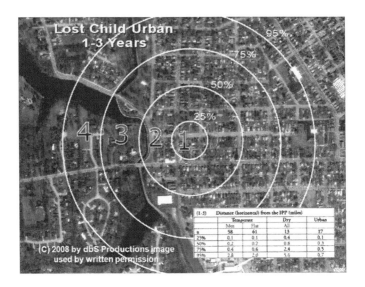

Lost Child Urban 1-3 Years

(1-3) Distance (horizontal) from the IPP (miles)			
	Temperate	Dry	Urban
	Mtn	Flat	All	
n	58	61	13	17
25%	0.1	0.1	0.4	0.1
50%	0.2	0.2	0.8	0.3
75%	0.4	0.6	2.4	0.5
95%	2.8	2.0	5.6	0.7

(C) 2008 by dbS Productions image used by written permission

Have the groups determine what locations they want to search first. The child's daycare center, parks, school playgrounds, and neighbor's houses with dogs are all good locations to look. Registered sex offenders in the area will be another concern that must be addressed by the groups. Using a few cheap props, students can learn how to effectively search for missing people and save lives.

As first graders, we were excited each Friday for *Show and Tell*. We could bring in a prop to impress our classmates (I brought in a cow's eyeball once), and we were intrigued to find out what they brought in to show us. Relevant props, like a map or fingerprint kit, are engaging by their very nature and will help you increase your audience participation.

Campfire Cops

Group discussions can be dominated by one or two members if you are not alert, and it can be difficult to notice when you have four or five groups to facilitate. This activity is based on the campfire method of taking turns when telling stories and it ensures everyone is involved.

For this example, we are using groups of six. Separate the topic handout onto six separate index cards, and hand one to each member of a group. Each student *must* take a turn reading their portion of the handout to the others. Only after every member has read their information can the group discussion begin. By using this method, each student is forced to add to the conversation.

For the topic *Child Abuse and Neglect Investigation,* we want our audience to leave with skills that they can use for interrogating suspects. I normally do not number the individual handouts, but I did so in this example to add clarity. Allowing students to figure out what order the information is applied can be a valuable part of the activity.

Understanding the Psychology of Child Molesters: A Key to Getting Confessions

©Police Chief Magazine – *Used with permission*

Group Member #1: Maryland Heights Study. In a 30-month period, from 2003 to 2005, the authors interviewed 45 convicted child molesters, both men and women, at several prisons in Missouri, as part of two separate research projects. Many of the offenders were true pedophiles, while others were more situational-type child molesters, individuals who took advantage of an opportunity to have sexual contact with a child. Collectively, these 45 offenders molested more than 350 children.

Group Member #2: Those who made admissions or confessions were asked to give their reasons for doing so. Those who did not make any admission of guilt were asked to explain why.

* 16 (36%) of the 45 offenders did not confess or make any admissions of guilt when interviewed by the police. Many of these offenders stated that they did not confess solely because of the way they were treated or questioned by the police.

* 29 (64%) of the 45 offenders confessed or at least made some admission of guilt when interviewed by the police. 18 (62%) of these 29 offenders acknowledged that although they made some admission, they withheld significant information, most often about undisclosed victims. One of the offenders

claimed that he had 73 previous victims that he never disclosed to the investigator and for which he was never prosecuted.

Group Member #3: *Understand the Thinking Process.* One of the critical keys to interviewing child molesters is to understand how they think. There are several different types of child molester; each child molester has a particular way to meet his or her needs and to justify his or her behavior. Molesters use distorted thinking to rationalize and justify their crimes, to make their own needs most important and to minimize their behavior. Many offenders convince themselves that the relationship they had with their victim was different; that it was a mutual, loving, caring relationship; that the sexual acts were consensual; or that the child somehow benefited from the relationship. The more an investigator understands the way a sexual offender thinks, the more prepared he will be to elicit a confession.

Group Member #4: During the investigative interview, a suspect might disclose his own history of childhood sexual abuse, trying to use it as a defense for his behavior. For example, the suspect might say, *"It happened to me; therefore, I would never do that to someone else."* In fact, rather than signaling a flat denial, a revelation like that should open the door for an investigator to explore how that sexual abuse might have affected the suspect's own sexual development. Many offenders will admit that their own victimization resulted in confusion and sexual experimentation during their teenage years. This line of questioning will sometimes help the offender to open up and admit to the offense he has committed.

Group Member #5: *Demonstrate Respect in the Interview.* The most consistent reason offered by the offenders for why they confessed their crime was the immediate and constant *"respect"* shown them by the interviewer. Respect meant several things to them. In some cases, the interviewer engaged in nonthreatening, nonspecific, non crime-related conversation. The interviewer clearly demonstrated a psychological understanding of sex offenders and was able to create a feeling that the interviewer, as one offender stated, *"cared about my issues and showed real concern for me as a human being."* One told us: *"He was the first policeman who ever treated me right. He made me feel like a real person, not a criminal."* Another said, *"I have been treated like shit* *by the police all of my life. I didn't think any of them were any good or gave a damn about anybody but themselves. When Detective ____ talked to me, he treated me like a man, not a kid. He was tough but fair, and never once did he ever talk down to me."*

Group Member #6: *Develop Rapport.* The second significant reason for confessing was the *"ease of conversation,"* and a perception that the interviewer quickly established trust and understanding and could provide them with help. Participants described how they were *"short-circuited,"* expecting a *"police bully"* but instead, finding the opposite and actually liking the interviewer. Conversation was easy; it was not difficult to confess to someone they perceived as a friend.

After each member reads their portion of the handout and the group has time to discuss the information, you can use any number of methods to conclude the group. You can lead a class discussion to wrap up the information, play a game, give a test, or have the groups quiz each other.

With this particular handout, I followed up by showing several videos of sex offenders caught in a sting by *Dateline: To Catch a Predator.* I had the students explain how they would interview each suspect based on the information learned in their group. They were fascinated with the knowledge they now possessed to interview sexual predators, and they were engaged by the videos of real suspects. Students were able to use the new information right away and could see a real world application.

Another great way to conclude *Campfire Cops* is by having the teams quiz one another after they study the handouts. Instruct each group to create five questions on what they have just learned. The students read the material, discuss it, study it, form it into a question, and are quizzed – all are effective methods for them to learn and retain information. You now have a test and competition in one. Each group will study hard to create challenging test questions for their peers, and prepare for the same.

> Students were able to use the new information right away and could see a real world application.

Games for Review and Retention

Everyone enjoys playing, especially our students who love to win at everything, and games provide a dynamic method for students to review their material. By using interactive games and group activities, you will become a three-dimensional trainer.

There are several interactive review games at *LEOtrainer.com/games*. Creative people with more computer skills than I possess designed these games – I simply adapted them for our purposes. The games on the website include *Jeopardy, Password*, and *Are You Smarter than a Rookie*. You can enter any

information you want into each game format and use it for a review, study session, or test. Split your students into groups to compete against each other, and watch as everyone continuously reviews the material to win the game. It is a refreshing method of retention for any class.

Puzzles are another format to consider using for a refreshing change of pace. Designing a word search, criss-cross, hidden message, or cryptogram is easier than ever before. Puzzlemaker is a free resource for educators under the "Teachers" link at www.discoveryeducation.com. You can use a puzzle during your presentation or provide several of them as a welcome alternative to studying notes. The program is simple to use, and your students will enjoy working *with* the information instead of repeatedly looking over the same notes, night after night.

SWAT Teams Review

My son, Richard, told me about a review game involving fly swatters when he was still in high school, and hearing him speak about the review with such enjoyment caused me to adapt it to serve our audience.

Students work individually with the support of a group during the activity. You will need three flyswatters and a handful of index

---

cards to get started. Write each answer to your review questions on a separate index card or a piece of paper.

Hang the answers on a wall in any order you like. One member from each team stands with their back to the wall with a *flySWATer* in hand (come on – that's funny). Once you ask the review question, the student who turns and hits the answer with the *flySWATer* first is awarded the point for their team. Rotate new players to the wall from each team after the question is answered.

Instruct the students who are sitting down to look for the answer in their notes just in case their teammate draws a blank. They should work together and coach their teammate (usually by yelling the answer).

At least two groups, or *SWAT Teams*, are required for this game. Three groups tend to be more engaging and humorous, but four teams can be crowded and hard to referee. To add interest, you can use pictures or images as clever answers.

> The activity is more effective than telling our students to study their notes because we ran out of material.

SWAT Teams is an interactive and competitive activity that creates an environment where everyone continuously studies the information to win the game. The activity is more effective than telling our students to study their notes because we ran out of material.

Just pick up a few flyswatters and you are in business. You can have three answers on the wall or thirty. It is up to you. Cadets will push and shove their way to the correct answer and laughter will fill the room. *SWAT Teams* is an exciting method for review but make sure you maintain some control. I am from the country so that means *no blood – no foul.*

Students Teach Students

We can increase our students' confidence by sharing the responsibility of teaching with them; it is one of the most effective techniques available to enhance learning. When students work on a problem and teach others the best method of resolution, they fully engage the lesson. It is underutilized because it is not always easy to employ in an academy or in-service setting.

It will always be important for instructors to demonstrate skills to their students, but we must ensure students can demonstrate them back in some measureable way. Cadets are only safe to transition from students to cops after they have proven that they can make choices decisively and act on them quickly. That is what separates the civilian world from law enforcement.

As an instructor, you first have to learn the material and prepare to teach it before you can present it to an audience. It provides you with a firm grasp of the information and quite often broadens your understanding through the process. If it works that way for you and me, it will work just as well for our students. It can be hard to surrender some of the control, but it will benefit our profession.

If you want the cadets to *understand* the *4 Ds of Crime Prevention,* having them copy the SPOs from the screen and testing them on the information will not accomplish that. Get students more involved by having them *discuss* and *instruct* the topic.

Start by having each cadet write down an example from their house, work place, or school for each of the *4 Ds: Deny, Delay, Detect,* and *Deter.* This simple activity helps them see past the definitions and requires them to connect the subject to policing. Place cadets into small groups where they can compare their examples with their peers.

Require each team to determine which of their combined examples best describes each of the *4 Ds,* and then instruct them to create a presentation representing them. Assign each group a different teaching method (chalk board, slide show, flip chart, role-play, demonstration, etc.) to use. Teams will be creative when challenged to use different resources, and students will appreciate the value in understanding and practicing the *4 Ds of Crime Prevention.*

"Experience: that most brutal of teachers. But you learn, my God do you learn." ~C. S. Lewis

Weakness vs. Integrity

I have heard it from cops, soldiers, and TV icons: *"When you apologize, it is a sign of weakness."* That makes as much sense as pre-moistened diapers to me, and it sounds like an excuse to be arrogant and indignant at the same time (neither of which are admirable). If you are apologizing before your presentation starts from a lack of preparation, it *is* a sign of weakness. That is not my focus here.

If we are truly mistaken, it is not a sign of weakness to apologize or to say that we are wrong. It does no one any good to dwell upon the mistake, but they will if we do not set the record straight. Our lack of integrity will be on their minds as we try to continue to teach, and it will become the topic of discussion during their break. It can destroy our connection with the audience and stop all participation if allowed to go unchecked.

If we are there for our audience, it should not be a problem to admit when we are wrong. Whenever I find myself falling back on the *"weakness"* argument, I know I have made it about me. We do not need to grovel or beg for forgiveness; we should acknowledge our error and get on with the presentation. You will garner more respect by admitting you are wrong than by showing students your PhD in the field. You can model strong character when you choose not to follow this misguided mindset and increase your audience's appreciation and participation.

> You will garner more respect by admitting you are wrong than by showing students your PhD in the field.

If you do not particularly like my assessment, you are welcome to ignore it, or if you are confronted with such a situation and find yourself suddenly overwhelmed by *weakness,* do not apologize again.

SPIM Factoid

SPIM can breathe underwater and drink coffee at the same time.

Spellbinding Lectures

Lectures are the backbone of the education system in America, and the police academy is no exception. While I like to highlight the increased value of active learning, the lecture will always have a place in the learning process. Lecture can be an excellent method to convey information when it is done well; however, active learning – which requires students to discover, discuss, demonstrate, and explain the information – is more suited to our audience. The two methods should be combined by the police instructor to create *Spellbinding Lectures*.

"I hear and I forget. I see, I remember.
I do, I understand." ~*Confucius*

Confucius was onto something. Knowing the learning styles of most cops and cadets, we can add to his declaration for the police instructor.

- When I only **hear** information, I may forget some. (Lecture)
- When I **hear** and **see** information, I will remember. (Add videos, pictures, and images to the lecture)
- When I **hear**, **see**, **discuss**, and **question** the information, I understand. (Add group exercises to the lecture)
- When I **demonstrate** and **teach** others the information, I become proficient and skillful. (Add students teaching exercises and activities to the lecture)

Lecturing is still the most efficient way to impart knowledge and communicate large amounts of material in a short amount of time, but that does not mean that everyone is retaining that knowledge, or is even awake. For the younger generation of law enforcers, who have grown up in an active world filled with attention-grabbing commercials and video games, a lecture can be painful.

Learning is not guaranteed just because we pour out information on a particular topic. Active lectures emphasize the real world in a classroom, something our audience needs. The involvement of our audience is necessary before any real learning can occur. With active involvement, the student is seeking an answer to a question, or information to solve a group problem, or a technique necessary to perform a skill.

> Learning is not guaranteed just because we pour out information on a particular topic.

Any teaching method can be good or bad depending on how that method is applied, and lecturing is the best possible method in some instances. We need to lecture with three learning domains in mind: the "head" (knowing), the "heart" (feeling), and the "hands" (doing).

Heads, Hearts, & Hands

Bloom's Taxonomy breaks the objectives into three domains: Cognitive, Affective, and Psychomotor.

Skills in the cognitive domain (the head), revolve around knowledge, comprehension, and critical thinking of a particular topic. Giving a quiz would require the student's to access their cognitive domain. Skills in the affective domain (the heart), include emotional reactions and empathy. Talking to cadets about the results of child abuse or another particularly emotional subject would rouse this domain. Skills in the psychomotor domain (the hands) are identified by the ability to physically manipulate a tool or instrument. Teaching a cadet the proper way to load and fire a gun would be one way to stimulate this domain.

Demonstrating for the class how to search a prisoner only reaches their cognitive domain (the head). But when the students demonstrate the same technique on each other, a psychomotor skill (the hands) can be developed. While skills associated with the psychomotor domain are retained at high levels in the brain, repetition is still the key. Showing a video of a jailer being stabbed by a prisoner who was poorly searched will also connect their affective domain (the heart) to round off the learning experience.

If you want to be effective as an instructor, think along the lines of *Bloom* when you are lecturing. If we involve these three areas in our lectures – using different techniques and exercises – we will produce a better class of guardians for society. This chapter will provide you with several concrete methods to do just that.

Law Enforcer Layout

Whether you are using a curriculum developed by you or someone else, it will benefit the audience if you follow some basic principles of layout. When you are giving a lecture to cops, think about how law enforcers like to receive information. The principles used for business and management do not always go over well with our brothers and sisters in blue, so make sure you custom fit any material for the benefit of law enforcers. I have seen dozens of checklists and design formats for lecturing; some are simplistic and others are complicated – I prefer a simple approach. The following is an example of the *Richipedia* process of lecture layout. As with everything else in this book, you can use it, modify it, or forget it.

The Dispatch: When you first start, give law enforcers a brief summary of major points you will cover during the lecture. Like a dispatch call for service, give them a *"heads up"* of what is coming their way. Provide them with an idea of how you will conclude and what benefits they will take with them at the end.

BOLO: Create themes or headlines for your main points or SPOs. Let the audience know there will be valuable information provided during your lecture, and they should *"Be On the Look Out"* for wisdom.

Modus Operandi: You must provide students with the *"mode of operating"* by giving real-life illustrations through case examples and analogies. You should use examples as often as possible with each topic – raw information can be confusing if you do not show law enforcers how it can be applied. Using videos from reality shows or dash cams is a powerful resource for *Modus Operandi.*

Physical Evidence: Your class will benefit from seeing your lecture come to life through a *PowerPoint* presentation, handouts, flip charts, and props. We are visual beings; we learn best when we have something to look at.

As part of the physical evidence, you need to actively involve students in the lecture through individual or group activities. The majority of our audience enjoys kinesthetic learning, and they want to get their hands on the information. Demonstrations and skill-building go hand-in-hand with police work and should go hand-in-hand with your lecture.

Spellbinding Visuals

Here are some of the issues created by traditional one-sided lectures (Johnson, Johnson, and Smith, 1991).

* Attention decreases with each passing minute of a lecture
* Only auditory learners are engaged
* Lower-level (only factual) learning is promoted

Lectures only become a problem when they are one-sided with no interaction from the audience. One master trainer (Pike, 2003) found that adding visuals to lectures resulted in a significant improvement in retention. It makes sense when you understand that between 80% and 90% of all information we absorb is visual

(Jensen, 2000). Research shows that using images and color is an effective way to get the brain's attention; color even enhanced memory. Farley and Grant (1976) showed that full color multi-media images promoted recall much better than black and white images. Jensen and Dabney (2000) showed that college students performed better when tests were printed on blue paper instead of red. The color blue is more calming than red and promotes deep thinking and concentration. Just the simple addition of visual aids can promote an increase in learning.

> Between 80% and 90% of all information we absorb is visual

Keep them Moving

Anytime we can get our students moving around, it increases their potential to learn and serves to keep their heads off the table – both are of interest to instructors. Dr. David A. Sousa is a consultant in educational neuroscience whose research has provided educators with strategies for improving student learning by simple physical interaction. *"It seems that the more we study the [brain], the more we realize that movement is inescapably linked to learning"* (Sousa, 2000). The *Richipedia* interpretation: Get cadets moving around, and it will kick their brains into gear.

"Today's brain, mind and body research establishes significant links between movement and learning. Educators ought to be purposeful about integrating movement activities into daily learning (Jensen, 1998)". This research should inspire us to keep our lecture active whether by having a cadet fill in the blanks on a worksheet or by having them demonstrate their newly acquired skills.

"By engaging active and emotional pathways (the 'how' and the 'wow'), we supply an additional 'hook' for learning." (Jensen and Dabney, 2000)." In other words, *physical activity* and *emotional content* activate more of the brain, and that enhances retention.

Spellbinding Questions

Build questions into your slide show to keep the audience attentive. Every few minutes, have a question appear on the screen for the class to answer; multiple choice questions serve the technique well.

Instead of asking questions throughout the lecture, you may choose to begin with a short quiz. Make sure you include a few quirky or controversial questions about the topic. Do not grade the quiz or give the correct answers, but challenge the students to listen for the answers during your lecture. Let them grade their own quiz as you teach the topic. At the end, use the quiz as a group discussion guide.

Students need to question, talk about, think through, argue, and recall your lecture to help the information fully sink in. Let them do the digging and research for important material. Whoever is working the hardest at learning will gain the most knowledge; that should be your students – not you.

"Lectures in which students are continuously asked to interact hold extra benefits for learning. Students get to test their understanding of the material as it is presented; they have repeated opportunities to use critical thinking and to be creative. Their motivation to study, research the topic, and keep up with assignments also improves (Bligh, 2000).*"*

Patrol Partners

Partnering up is a quick and easy way to involve everyone in the audience. When your topic does not allow enough time for other activities, have students partner up with the person sitting next to them. It helps cadets form a personal bond with one of their peers as they discuss the topic, research a handout together, respond to a question, or compare their work. They learn to count on each other and trust others for back-up, a valuable lesson for law enforcers.

Placing questions throughout your slide show works well with *Patrol Partners.* Each time a question comes up, let the pairs quickly discuss their answer and check their notes before you choose someone to answer.

Quiz Five-O Style

Start by telling your students "there will be several quizzes throughout my lecture today," and require them to take notes that they can refer back to when taking the quizzes. Challenge them to recognize and take detailed notes of all relevant information – not just the SPOs – a skill they will need later when interviewing victims, witnesses, and suspects.

Give your lecture in chunks of 30 to 60 minutes and then stop for a *Quiz Five-0 Style*. Hand each cadet a blank index card and instruct them to write down one test question about the topic. Collect all the cards; shuffle them, and have students take turns drawing a card for a unique and interactive review.

Instruct each cadet to read their question out loud and give them 15 seconds to consult their notes and answer. Reward any correct answer with points or prizes (the goofier the better). I use toy police officers (like toy soldiers) and call them *Officer Neil* action figures. Cadets are competitive, and when the activity becomes a competition with prizes, they will scan their notes to create complex questions to stump their classmates.

Students will be on the edge of their seats during each chunk of your lecture looking to create formidable questions. For a more intense review, continue to give a prize for correct answers, but additionally require pushups, sit-ups, or some other consequence (determined by the class) for wrong answers. If a student answers incorrectly and owes some pushups to the class, the cadet who wrote the question gets the prize.

Every once in a while I change the rules to keep it interesting and fresh. For an easy adjustment, have one student read the question out loud and then let them choose another cadet to answer it. If the chosen student answers correctly, they both get a prize, but if not, they are doing pushups together.

Cadets thrive when they are challenged to think and pressured to perform. They have to actively listen, take notes, formulate test questions, contemplate answers, and speak in front of a group.

Once the activity is over, keep the index cards as an added bonus. Students will pose questions you never thought about asking in ways you never thought about asking them. You may find some of these questions useful to challenge future students or include in your next presentation. *Quiz Five-0* is always engaging for the audience, and it will provide you with plenty of laughs and new material as you facilitate the activity.

Police Briefing

Divide the students into small teams, and then have each group form a U-shape so every member is able to see your presentation. Before you begin, advise them to take thorough notes for an assignment that follows the lecture. Teach in chunks of 30 to 45 minutes (choosing logical points to stop at). Have each cadet write down a brief summary of the chunk that you just presented. Create some pressure by limiting their time to one minute. Now the group work begins.

Have the cadets go around their group and read their summaries. Have them determine which ideas and words illustrate the information in a concise and clear way. Instruct each group to develop a one-minute *Police Briefing* using their combined notes. Give them a few minutes to complete the short report that must include an *original* example. Allow them one minute to present their report to the class. Groups must designate a new speaker each time they present a briefing.

This technique keeps everyone tuned in to your lecture. They learn to pull out the relevant information – a skill they will need when they interview people in the real world. They hear it, write it, discuss it, and teach it.

Some students will zone out when material other than the SPOs are being covered. They decide that only the SPOs count for the test, so why not ignore the rest. The information between the SPOs can be just as important to their success as a cop – even more so at times – and this type of activity will ensure they pay attention to those details that they might normally ignore.

Once you see how effective it can be, it is tempting to use this method all the time. The *Police Briefing* technique can be adapted to fit shorter topics, roll call briefings, or in-service training.

Tactical Training Squads

With the *Tactical Training Squads,* each student researches and discusses the topic, learns from several other group members, and teaches other students. Depending on the depth of your material, the activity can last from 30 to 90 minutes.

This example is based on the 4 Steps of Problem Solving, the SARA Model. Separate the class into four equal *Study Groups* giving each group a handout with only *one* of the four steps involved in the model: Scanning, Analysis, Response, or Assessment. One cadet in each group will read the handout to their group members who must concentrate on taking notes. The group will then discuss the meaning of their step and its possible law enforcement applications. Have them focus on picking out the relevant information for their notes – not copying the entire handout word for word.

Study Groups

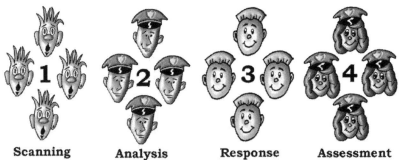

| Scanning | Analysis | Response | Assessment |

You may consider having the groups stand up while taking their notes – like they will as an officer taking a report. Let them know that they will not only be responsible for teaching the information to other students, but they will also be tested. That way each member has the responsibility to take notes and contribute. Here is the abbreviated assignment for each of the groups:

SARA Model Tactical Training Squad Exercise

The problem: Daytime drug deals are taking place in the community park across from the local high school. Dealers, addicts, and drug waste are a problem. Try to understand and apply your part of the SARA Model.

GROUP #1: SCANNING – This is where problems are identified. First, engage the group in brainstorming a list of problems (dangers of drug trafficking, gang involvement, violent crime, etc...). Some potential sources of information are:

* Patrol officers, Detective Division, Crime Analysis, Crime Prevention Unit, etc.
* Local Businesses
* Churches
* Schools
* Other Associations
* Surveys
* List other sources you might use for identifying crime problems.

Once a problem list has been assembled, consolidated, and then prioritized, the scanning step is complete.

GROUP #2: ANALYSIS – Human nature is to go from the identification of a problem to a response without knowing the details. This step in the SARA model, searching and evaluating the details, is the heart of the problem-solving process. The information gathered must be thorough and from a variety of sources. Do not rely strictly on the police for information regarding the crime issue. Make sure you understand the problem from the perspectives of the key stakeholders in the neighborhood, and be sure to identify the underlying nature of the problem through a complete analysis of the data. When you understand all parts of the problem, design a tailored response.

GROUP #3: RESPONSE – Clarify, and if necessary, redefine the problem before initiating the team's response. Make sure you have solicited suggestions for a solution to a particular problem from sources outside your group. Remember that not all solutions are designed to eliminate the problem entirely.

* What will be the goal(s) of your response toward the problem? What do you hope to accomplish by addressing this problem?
* What strategies will be used to meet the goal(s)?

✯ Will you eliminate, reduce, displace, prevent, or do something else with the problem?

✯ Concentrate on the individuals causing the problem.

✯ Organize and work with citizens.

GROUP #4: ASSESSMENT – How will you know if you accomplished your goal? It is important to go back after a period of time and evaluate your results. Some of the ways you assess may need to be considered before this step. For instance, if you are dealing with gang graffiti, you may want to take before and after photographs of some of the areas where the problem exists. For another problem, you may solely rely on statistics and numbers like those used in traffic enforcement studies. This stage is often forgotten or ignored. Groups can become so committed to their solution that they are reluctant to consider a newer or better option.

Once the *Study Group* time is up, take away the handouts so all the students have to reference are their notes. If they failed to take good notes, they will soon learn a valuable lesson. Form *Tactical Training Squads* of four members by joining people from each of the original Scanning, Analysis, Response, and Assessment groups. One at a time, the students will instruct the other squad members on their step of the SARA Model and lead a group discussion about the step's importance.

Each of the *Tactical Training Squads* must understand *The 4 Steps of Problem Solving* and figure out in what order the steps must be used. They will apply the model on the drug problem in the park, and present their plan to the rest of the class.

As the instructor you will act as a facilitator, so do not leave the room or read the newspaper. Take the time to walk around and listen to their conversations. Encourage groups when you hear a good idea or guide them back if they get off topic. You should allow 20 to 45 minutes for this portion of the activity, depending on the complexity of the information.

They have heard the information, determined what was relevant, written it down, discussed it with a *Study Group*, taught the information to their *Tactical Training Squad*, discussed it more, and now they must present it as a team.

Tactical Training Squads will challenge your students as they take on the individual responsibility to learn, participate in a group, and act as an instructor.

High Definition or Analog – Both Work

Many of our colleagues already strive to create *Spellbinding Lectures*. Randy is an instructor who makes the extra effort to engage his students. Serving law enforcement with Ohio's Department of Natural Resources provides him with unique experiences that are interesting and relevant. Our first meeting came when he fell ill while in the middle of teaching the 24-hour block on *Community Diversity* for a night academy. I was only stepping in for a few hours but he contacted me to let me know where he left off and what he planned on covering. He was concerned about his class under a substitute's control and wanted to ensure that it would be persuasive and engaging until his return. He left materials for me and marked the lesson plan where he had stopped the prior evening. He set everything up for my success to ensure the cadets would benefit from my fill-in role. It was refreshing to hear from an instructor who was passionate about teaching, and I would soon find out just how passionate he truly was.

I arrived an hour early to look over his materials and decide how to incorporate them into my presentation. I was shocked to find a cart stacked with Tupperware boxes when I arrived. They were filled with VHS tapes, books, CDs, flyers, and handouts. All just for the *Diversity* block! I have invested hundreds of hours compiling videos, images, and materials to teach the topic, but I think he has me beat. I like to convert everything into a digital format and keep it all on my laptop, but Randy prefers the hard copy approach. His methods are just as effective as mine and the students are intrigued by his style of delivery.

Students are interested whenever they see an instructor bring in their own materials. When Randy walks in with several boxes of information, he has captured their attention before he even begins. Students know when they are learning from an instructor who puts great effort into preparing a presentation, and they are compelled when he teaches diversity as a survival course instead of lecturing them about tolerance. Randy knows the topic well and that results in a powerful delivery – he is a model for other instructors to follow. You do not have to be computer savvy to create *Spellbinding Lectures* – just dedicated.

A Nuclear Physicist's Take on Lecture

Enrico Fermi (1901–1954) was an Italian-American physicist known for the development of the first nuclear reactor. He also made contributions to the development of quantum theory, nuclear physics, and statistical mechanics. He was awarded the 1938 Nobel Prize in Physics for his work on induced radioactivity. Fermi is widely regarded as one of the leading scientists of the

20th century, and along with Robert Oppenheimer, he is frequently referred to as *the father of the atomic bomb*. All-in-all, he sounds like a smart guy. After attending a Physics lecture at the University of Chicago, he stated: *"Before coming here, I was confused about this subject. Having listened to your lecture, I'm still confused, but on a higher level."*

The essence of training is creating an experience that will provoke thought and learning. Training should be about learning the realities of law enforcement – not just learning information to pass a test. Real training cannot take place when the audience is asked to do nothing. A lecture must be conducted with the audience in mind, or anyone can feel lost, even a genius who is capable of inventing a nuclear bomb.

The Spice of Life

Consider using a variety of methods in your lecture. You can combine the *Police Briefing*, *Tactical Training Squads*, and *Quiz Five-0 Style* to provide cadets with a compelling lesson. Variety is the spice of life and the spice of *Spellbinding Lectures*. You can *trick out* your lecture and captivate any law enforcement audience by using the examples, techniques, exercises, and methods throughout this book.

> *"It is not because things are difficult that we do not dare; it is because we do not dare that they are difficult."*
> ~Seneca

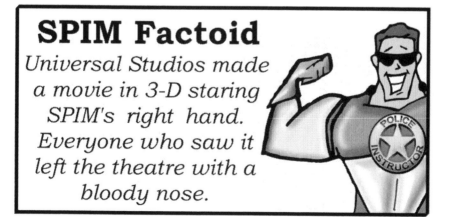

SPIM Factoid
Universal Studios made a movie in 3-D staring SPIM's right hand. Everyone who saw it left the theatre with a bloody nose.

Speech Design & Delivery

I saw him draw a gun from his waist and then, bang, bang, bang. *"Oh crap, I'm hit!"* I could feel the sting when the round struck my left hand. It stung worse than I expected but I kept moving and fired back. I only had eight rounds, so I had to make them count, and the wide open field offered no cover. I stayed on the move to make myself a hard target. He finally dropped when I landed two rounds to his head, and I ran over and rubbed it in, *"Better learn to shoot and move if you want to live rookie."*

It was a training exercise at the range using our Simunitions training system. The wax rounds delivered more reality than any other type of firearms training that I had participated in. I was a field training officer paired up with my recruit for the exercise, who had just bragged about how high he scored during qualification on the range. He was a great shot but he just received a taste of stress and reality. The exercise was restricted to an area twenty feet square. He was allowed to draw and fire first, but his first round was a miss. Once I returned fire, he turned his head and fired wildly – only hitting me once in the hand. I landed all eight rounds, 6 to the chest and 2 to the head. The red splatter marks on his face shield surprised him, and he tripped while trying to back pedal. You could see how shocked he was that a training simulation, or game, could be so stressful.

Law enforcers understand the benefits of stress testing in training. It is how we push ourselves past normal limits so we can withstand the anxiety and pressures of policing. It creates a unique form of determination in cops that few others share. *So I ask you, how stressful is speaking in front of other people compared to police work?*

The next morning I received a phone call from the captain. He told me the chief of police was expected to deliver a speech to the Rotary Club, but he was busy. He wanted me to fill in. I replied with the only acceptable answer, "Okay?" I was a little surprised when told the meeting was in a few hours. The room would be filled with business people and politicians from around the city, and I had no slides or handouts to carry me through. I had a short amount of time to prepare so there was no time to whine about how unfair the situation was.

The training from the day before turned out to be a good reminder that the speech was not my biggest worry as a cop. I was in a profession filled with stressful situations and things that went wrong all the time, yet I had survived. What was the worst thing that could happen while giving a speech at a luncheon? No one in the audience was going to spit on me or try to assault me regardless of my platform skills.

I jotted down a few key points and talked about each one for a few minutes. I was comfortable since I had no time to memorize a speech or worry about which items should be left in or taken out. I spoke about my police experience and based the talk on ideas and beliefs I held on the topic. I mixed in some humor that came to mind and then sat down.

"Be sincere; be brief; be seated" ~*Franklin D. Roosevelt*

I was asked back by the club more than a dozen times after that first presentation. I was simply having a conversation, and they liked it. It is nice to have time to prepare, but you already have hundreds of speeches floating around in your head if you are confronted with a similar situation.

Great Examples of Public Speaking

Lt. Col. Dave Grossman (Ret.), the author of *On Combat*, provides a great example of how to speak to law enforcers or any audience for that matter. He is a former Army Ranger, professor of psychology at West Point, and a nationally recognized scholar on aggression. He travels the nation training our military and law enforcement warriors about human aggression and violent crime. He is a compelling speaker because he talks about his experience, his passion, his ideas, and his understanding of the topic. He does not try to talk like a professor teaching down to subordinate students, but as a friend sharing wisdom.

Grossman had no notes or papers in his hands – only a microphone and a marker for flip charts. He gestured constantly using his entire body – not just his hands. He strolled back and forth across the stage and wandered out into the audience. He constantly asked for comments from the attendees and wrote them down on one of several flip charts in the room. He earnestly conveyed his convictions and was not afraid to share his beliefs with anyone.

When you choose to speak on a topic that is felt by the heart and well thought out by the mind, the audience will be engaged. By putting yourself into a speech, your presentation will become dynamic for you and your audience.

Another speaker to observe and learn from is Gavin de Becker, the

> When you choose to speak on a topic that is felt by the heart and well thought out by the mind, the audience will be engaged.

Police Instructor © 2011

author of *The Gift of Fear*. He is the leading expert on fear and how to assess the likelihood of violence. While less animated than the Colonel, he is still passionate about his topic and convincing through his delivery. He frequently stands at the lectern and refers to his notes, but he never reads a speech word for word or tries to memorize it. De Becker knows his material and talks about ideas through stories: he does not fixate on words.

You can watch video clips of each presenter (and several others) by visiting *LEOtrainer.com/speaking*. Once there, compare the different delivery styles to see how each speaker presents their information. More importantly, notice how both are equally engaging and compelling teachers.

Become a Rookie Again

You do not need to copy or mimic someone else, but you can always learn from watching others and incorporate certain techniques you find appealing. A new recruit will ride with four or five different FTOs during their training period and develop their own unique style. In the same manner, you should pick out the best of each speaker you see and develop your own style when delivering a speech. You should only seek to enhance your delivery by adding new skills and techniques – not by changing who you are.

Do Not Read or Memorize a Speech

I recently attended an academy graduation where I heard two speeches. One was delivered by a school administrator and the other by an officer – both had me wanting to gouge my ears with a hot poker.

They surely meant well as they thanked everyone in the room, and I mean everyone. They each read their speech word for word which forced them into a monotone state that would put anyone to sleep. The educator looked up from his speech several times but always stared at the same point on the wall. He never scanned the crowd or made eye contact with anyone. There was no emotion in his voice that might connect him to the graduating cadets or audience, and every line in his speech was an old cliché.

The cop was even worse. He looked up once during his speech and lost his place momentarily. I could see the frantic look on his face as he searched for the correct spot. That was the last time I saw his face until he was done with his eight minute recitation. I am positive he put great effort into his speech, but the theme was completely lost as he rambled through without ever pausing between sentences, paragraphs, or points. There was no indication when one point ended and the next began. His big mistake was leaving his experiences and beliefs out of his speech. He never talked about anything he had intimate experience with – and it showed.

After the first minute the audience started leaning their heads back and rolling their eyes. The cadets managed to keep their composure with the educator, but even they started to grimace with their law enforcement counterpart. Why do people chain themselves to a speech by reading it word for word or attempting to memorize it? It is an ineffective method of delivery and boring to boot. Have confidence in yourself and speak without memorization or reading word for word.

The best speech of the graduation came from one of the academy commanders. He was there to introduce the speakers and hand out certificates, but something popped into his head that he wanted to share. He walked away from the lectern and approached the cadets in the front row. You could see in their faces that they were completely engaged as he talked to them. He walked back and forth across the stage, and looked at each cadet as he gave them heartfelt advice.

> He walked away from the lectern and approached the cadets in the front row.

Within one minute, the commander brought laughter to the entire audience and nearly made the graduates cry. He did not *wing it,* he knew his material well. How? He spoke about his experiences as a law enforcer and gave advice that had been etched into his conscience. The commander was having a conversation. He focused on an idea and let the words come naturally – he did not need a speech.

I talked about the error made when trying to memorize your material in the chapter on *Planning & Preparation Shortcuts*, but I want to emphasize it again. Even for a short speech lasting only minutes, it is a mistake to try and memorize word for word. You will find yourself concentrating on words instead of your audience and the ideas you want them to walk away with.

Passion is far more important, in my opinion, than perfection. Like me, you may find that *off the cuff* thoughts provide your speech with vigor and vitality. These types of ideas, and the words that accompany them, help to provide your audience with a conversational experience they will not forget.

> Passion is far more important, in my opinion, than perfection.

Base Your Speech on Personal Experience

Whenever you speak in public, talk about something you are entitled to give an opinion on. Regardless of the topic, you should be able to find a real example from your law enforcement career (or personal life) to insert into the speech. It is much easier to talk about events you are familiar with than those taken from other sources.

When you are developing a speech ask yourself a few questions.

☆ Do I *believe* in what I am saying? Am I passionate about sharing my beliefs and experiences on the subject?

☆ Do I have proof or personal experience to back up what I am telling my audience? Can I give them examples to show it?

☆ If I am confronted by angry audience members can I easily defend my position? Would I want to?

If you cannot answer these questions without doubt in your mind, you need to make some changes to your speech. Talk to the audience about the lessons life has taught you as a law enforcer, and provide them with a valuable lesson in exchange for their time. Speakers who talk about the everyday conflicts of life never fail to keep the attention of their listeners. It does not matter how trivial your experience was at the time – people are compelled by stories they can relate to.

Only you know what you are passionate about. If you speak about your passions instead of trying to mimic a speech you heard somewhere else, the audience will be your devoted listeners. If you choose to speak about something you know little about, or have little interest in, you will not entertain anyone. If you are not impressed by the topic, your audience will know and soon share in your mood.

> If you choose to speak about something you know little about, or have little interest in, you will not entertain anyone.

Speak about the struggles that you had to overcome to make it into our profession. Have you met a great person who taught you a lesson? Are you an expert in a unique field? Have you studied a subject for years that you can provide valid insight on? Have you fought to survive – literally? Have you questioned your faith in times of stress?

Like most cops, you have the makings of a great speech for any occasion. Start writing down some of your experiences at the end of the chapter, and create a collection of speech topics from which to choose.

As a public speaker, your individuality is your most valuable commodity. It provides you with realism that adds power to any speech. Help the audience see what you saw, hear what you heard, feel what you felt, and learn what you learned.

Talk Like You Are 4 Again

When it comes to public speaking, we tend to get worse as we get older. We worry more about what people will think of our performance and less about what they get from our message. My mother claims it was nearly impossible to shut me up when I was four years old (some would say it's still true), and the same may have been said by your mother as well. That is because when we learned something new, we were passionate about sharing the experience with the world. We launched into every speech with reckless abandon and spoke with earnest conviction from our heart. It is that passion we need to recapture as adults.

Also at four, we were animated with our presentation as we tried to put our experience into words others could understand. Every facet of our personality was on display from the start. We did not waste time with formalities or start by telling a joke – we jumped right into our story and made a plea for understanding from our audience. We did not worry about our limitations or lack of training as a speaker. We had something important to say and we let our passion create a dynamic delivery.

Think of the last time a four year old tried to convince you of something – anything. Were they dramatic? Were they animated? Were they sincere and passionate? Unless they are from another planet, I will assume your answers were all *yes*. Next time you see them, ask for a few pointers on dynamic delivery skills. If you are short on time, allowing them to drink a *Vault* will speed up the lesson.

Make the Talk Clear & Concise

You only have so much time to deliver a speech. Your material needs to fit within limits and still be understood. One of the speeches I described earlier in this chapter lasted for eight minutes and covered 16 points of information. That is 30 seconds for each point he tried to make. Does that sound like a winning combination to you? Putting in an overabundance of information is just as bad as not preparing at all. They will not be impressed that you squeezed in so much material – just confused.

Most five minute speeches will have no more than two or three points supporting the overall theme. The only reason to have a point is to support your message. If it does not support the message, it does not belong in your speech.

Create Suspense

Try to create suspense during your speech, and there is no better time than the beginning. Think of ways to tell a personal story that allows for suspense to build causing your audience to eagerly wait for the conclusion.

The following is an example from a speech I delivered to a group of cadets on courage. I wanted them to think of courage in a different way than before, and I needed a real story that had a real outcome they could not argue with. I found the perfect one.

"We need people of courage to serve as law enforcers, but how do we measure such courage? You must have enough courage to fight and even kill to be called a hero. You cannot be a conscientious objector and a courageous warrior at the same time. Take this soldier from WWII that one unit had to bear.

When Desmond Doss was drafted, he filed to be a conscientious objector. He refused to kill, or carry a weapon into combat, because of his personal beliefs as a Seventh-day Adventist. He became a medic and served in the Pacific Theatre with the U.S. Army. His fellow soldiers despised him for being a coward and no one wanted to serve beside him. Can you blame them? These are the types of people who get cops and soldiers killed!

The 77th infantry was in a terrible fight in the Ryukyu Islands near Okinawa. They were attacking a 400-foot-tall cliff when they were torn apart by machine gun, mortar, and artillery fire. Seventy-five casualties were left behind as everyone withdrew, and there went the cowardly objector running away from the unit like you would expect. What do you think happened to all those men once the 77th withdrew?"

Are you interested in hearing the rest of the story? Are you eager to know more about the coward who ran away or what happened to the other soldiers? So was my class. You build suspense for your audience by the way you structure your story. You can hold their attention and heighten their curiosity, and they cannot help but become involved in your speech (another *Ninja*

Instructor Skill for you to use). To satisfy your curiosity, I will give you the rest of Doss's story.

Desmond Doss ran away from his unit, and back into the field of fire where he rescued all seventy-five casualties – alone. He pulled each of them to the edge of the cliff and lowered them down one by one to friendly hands. He had no assistance in the amazing feat of bravery, and Doss did not stop there.

He would go on to rescue many more on the field of battle and was injured several times himself. He was the first conscientious objector to receive the Congressional Medal of Honor in WWII. He also received three Purple Hearts and two Bronze Stars to round out his hero collection.

So what does it really mean to be courageous? It is not fighting or killing – Desmond did neither and he is without question courageous. It is about doing the right thing in spite of your fear, not about how you do it. As an officer, you become courageous when you choose to believe that the safety of our society is more important than your fear.

"Courage is being scared to death... and saddling up anyway." ~John Wayne

Chart Your Speech

As with any good voyage, you need to map out the course of your talk. I provide the illustration at the end of the chapter to outline a speech I delivered at an academy graduation. My message was *"Keys to Success for Law Enforcement Warriors."* My main points are on the notes and each item of information points to them. I do not need to add anything more on my stories because they are *my* stories. If I cannot fit everything on one sheet of paper, I know it is too much for a short speech. I have placed the *blank* format at *LEOtrainer.com/speaking* if you find it helpful when preparing for a speech of your own.

Speech Design & Delivery Tips

☆ Choose a topic you earnestly want to talk about.

☆ Limit your speech to one theme, and use 3 to 5 main points to support it.

☆ Use Post-it notes to help you move ideas around and organize your speech.

☆ Fill your talk with examples and illustrations.

☆ Add details to your stories, and allow your audience to relive the experiences you describe.

☆ Personalize your speech with information about the audience.

☆ Use familiar words so the audience understands you.

☆ Plan out your speech and rehearse your delivery.

☆ Skip the formalities and jump into your talk.

☆ Create suspense or drama to *hook* them.

☆ Tell the audience what you want them to take away and challenge them to do something.

☆ Close with a powerful statement and sit down.

"The art of war is a science in which nothing succeeds
which has not been calculated and thought out."
~Napoleon

SPIM Factoid
The UFC fights in a cage to keep SPIM out.

Keys to Success for LE Warriors

Before us sit the newest members of the Thin Blue Line. Part of a courageous warrior culture in our nation, willing to put everything on the line for justice and the safety of others. In my opinion, that is what makes them better than those who sit at Starbucks and complain about what's wrong with our world, but will never do anything about it. These are men and women of action.

I want to share with you keys to success that I learned during my career. A career in which I was repeatedly blessed and honored to be called a police officer.

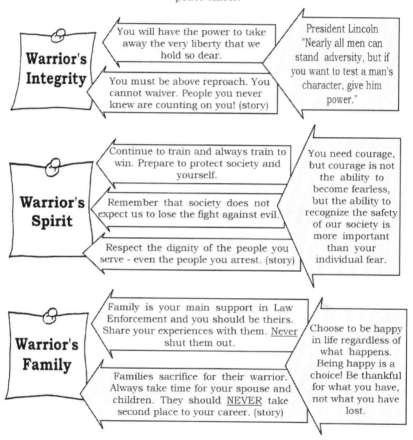

Warrior's Integrity

You will have the power to take away the very liberty that we hold so dear.

You must be above reproach. You cannot waiver. People you never knew are counting on you! (story)

President Lincoln "Nearly all men can stand adversity, but if you want to test a man's character, give him power."

Warrior's Spirit

Continue to train and always train to win. Prepare to protect society and yourself.

Remember that society does not expect us to lose the fight against evil.

Respect the dignity of the people you serve - even the people you arrest. (story)

You need courage, but courage is not the ability to become fearless, but the ability to recognize the safety of our society is more important than your individual fear.

Warrior's Family

Family is your main support in Law Enforcement and you should be theirs. Share your experiences with them. Never shut them out.

Families sacrifice for their warrior. Always take time for your spouse and children. They should NEVER take second place to your career. (story)

Choose to be happy in life regardless of what happens. Being happy is a choice! Be thankful for what you have, not what you have lost.

You will need the INTEGRITY, SPIRIT, & FAMILY OF A LEO WARRIOR.

This is the life that YOU chose. It's not risk free, nor will it be easy, but in the humble opinion of this proud police officer, it has always been a life well worth living. There is no more noble profession than the one you are now a member of.

I want to welcome you to our family with one final quote from Teddy Roosevelt: *"In any moment of decision, the best thing you can do is the right thing, the next best thing you can do is the wrong thing & the worst thing you can do is nothing."*

Confessions of a Police Instructor

I thought long and hard about adding this chapter to the book before finally working up the courage to include it. Cops are not always good at being transparent with their personal lives and I am no exception, but I believe our mission as police instructors must be based on honesty – so here it goes.

I Wrote for Selfish Reasons

I have selfish reasons for wanting our police instructors to get better and improve the safety of our law enforcers and the society they serve. With frequent visits to the Cleveland Clinic, I have come to the realization that I will not live to be a ripe old age. I have a vested interest in the next generation of police officers who will become the guardians that protect my wife and kids (maybe grandkids) after I am gone. We do not hesitate to invest in life insurance to protect our families – should we not also invest in our law enforcers who will provide a lifetime of vital service for them? This book is my investment in the development and training of worthy protectors to watch over my family and yours.

I want the best possible men and women wearing the badge when my loved ones need their help, and I want input on how they are trained. I want to make sure standards are kept high and that only the most qualified cadets with large quantities of integrity and humility are accepted. My family has been blessed by our profession, but they have also suffered through fear and pain because of it. Spending time writing the book, designing the website, and creating resources to help instructors could never repay their sacrifice, but I hope it will create a better world for them to live in when I am gone.

> This book is my investment in the development and training of worthy protectors to watch over my family and yours.

I Am a Jealous Instructor

I am jealous of every cop and cadet I teach. I loved being a police officer and was not ready to retire when my career ended; I still find myself wanting to take their place each time I talk about the unique profession we serve. Recently, while giving a speech during a graduation ceremony, I admitted my jealousy to the recruits and their families. I hope it served as a reminder of just how addictive this profession can be and what an honor it is to serve others as one of God's guardians of justice.

If you are still serving as a law enforcer, you should know that there are people that long to fill your shoes. In my two decades of policing, I served on the road patrol, as a crime scene investigator, as a criminal investigator, and as a school resource officer. I was blessed with a multitude of experiences while serving with three great organizations, and I overlooked how fortunate I had been until it was gone. And it was gone without warning.

What I missed the most were the people that made up the police division – not the building, the badge, or the cars (okay, the cars are pretty cool). The people stood beside me, shoulder to shoulder, while I went from one hospital to the next. They donated tens-of-thousands of dollars in sick time so my family never missed a pay check, and they never asked for a *thank you*. There is no profession quite like ours.

I was truly lost for a while, but finally realized I still had an oath to God to fulfill. To *protect and serve* His people is still my duty – I just accomplish it in a different way.

Like many of you, I did more to help others in one week than some people will do in a lifetime. That is the blessing of law enforcement, but it also comes with an addiction and its own form of withdrawals. By helping to develop the next generation of guardians, I find the symptoms are more bearable. It does not always feel as significant as being on the street, but I know it is.

I Am a Stingy Instructor

While attending a train-the-trainer course, I met several new instructors from all over Ohio. A few of them had no idea where to start; the course simply provided them with a lesson plan but not much more. I had accumulated a wealth of resources and information that could help them get started, but I found myself reluctant to share.

I had a hard time giving out my training materials to others unless they had something to offer in return. I made a rule – only give help to instructors and cops that worked hard to make the profession better – no one else. I finally realized the error of my ways and now *try* to encourage everyone, including those we might consider to be *slouches,* to become a better trainer. It can only improve our profession if someone shows them how to be more engaging and effective.

One officer was new to teaching, and I gave her copies of some videos, pictures, *PowerPoint* presentations, and resources that I had collected. It felt good when I helped her, and I felt guilty for not doing something sooner. Several other instructors also asked for materials, and I found myself burning discs each night of the class for someone different. By the final day, everyone was exchanging presentations with one another. Methods from Cleveland ended up in Dayton, and techniques from Hocking Hills are now taught in Bowling Green. We benefited more from the exchange of ideas than we did from the course.

My real fear was that I would become boring or mediocre if I gave all my ideas and hard work away. I feared walking into a class and finding the audience had already experienced one of my techniques. In fact, it happened, but the students were not restless or bored – they were attentive and engaged because they liked the technique. It benefited the students, and that is what is most important.

Just recently, I was tested again. I was co-teaching a class on *Crime Scene Search* with a new instructor. He had not taught the topic before and I was there to help him. I brought a cart full of props and evidence to create realistic crime scenes for the class, but he told me that he wasn't interested in doing that. I reminded him that the search was a required part of the curriculum to which he responded *"They only have a few weeks left."* I was surprised by the statement and assured him that we were setting up the crime scenes. I explained to him that the academy expected us to actively train the class even if there were only a few minutes left. I went to stage the scenarios in another room while he covered the SPOs.

When I returned to the classroom, the cadets looked at me as if they were prisoners. One student even mouthed *"help us."* The instructor was reading a page from the state's curriculum as if it were a book – something I had not seen since my days in the academy. The students went on break, and I asked him why he was reading the outline to the class. He replied *"No one gave me anything else."* He decided it was not his responsibility to be prepared, so I took over the classroom portion as well and then he sat down and started to read a magazine. I was ticked!

We made it through the class, and the cadets all processed a crime scene as required. He took a topic that was interactive by its very nature and made it a complete bore. I wanted to tell the instructor how much of a disappointment he was to our craft, but I did not. I knew once the commander heard about the class he would not allow the instructor to teach at his academy again, but I was sure that the man would find a position somewhere.

Instead of telling him what I thought, I gave him my slide show for *Crime Scene Search*. I told him to add cases and information of his own to personalize it for his next class. I wanted to *wash* my hands of him, but I knew he would teach again someday and have an effect on our profession. It did not feel good to give him anything, but it did feel right.

> It did not feel good to give him anything, but it did feel right.

When I used to worry about giving away my stuff and how it might affect my *persona* as an instructor, I was focusing on me and only me. Instead of concerning myself with our cadets, our officers, and our society, I worried about my ego, my pride, and my vanity. I encountered all of these obstacles again while writing *Police Instructor*, but this time I overcame them – I have a new mission.

I Gave Up in the Most Uninspiring Way

The doctor walked into my hospital room and said, *"Mr. Neil, I cannot figure out how to stop your pain, and you cannot go on like this much longer. I am going to send you home on some strong narcotics that should sedate you and help with the pain."* I was completely speechless (a rare occasion), but my wife Gloria asked *"Who should we see next?"* The doctor looked offended as if an accusation was made against her intellect. She responded *"Well I do not know what anyone else could do, but you can call whomever you like."* I went home and tried to hide my self-pity while I thought of ways to die with dignity. I simply gave up and was completely defeated in body and spirit. Fortunately for me, my family went along for the ride and they did not give up so easily.

I do not want anyone to think I am without my faults, or that I never give up. The fact is I did. I felt like a burden to my wife and kids, and I wondered what kind of father and husband I could be in a drug induced stupor. That is a glimpse of what my family has endured, and I had to apologize to them for the way I let them down.

Our friends and family would tell you that I am the noisy and overprotective city cop, and that Gloria is the devout Christian mother, wife, and friend. But fortunately for me, she also grew up *Pentecostal* and knew how to raise her voice when it mattered most. She was not about to let me get away with dying and leaving her alone to raise two teenagers. She ignored the doctor and called the Cleveland Clinic. There was no availability but the specialist saw me anyway just to stop Gloria from constantly harassing him with phone calls. She saved my life by not giving up on me – even though I gave up on myself. I thank God for her, and I realize that this book would not exist without her courage and continued sacrifice. That is why *Police Instructor* is dedicated to my family and yours.

I Feel Sorry for Myself

It's embarrassing to admit, but I feel sorry for myself – daily sometimes. My nerve damage was catastrophic and the debilitating pain caused by my injury is constant. I have 4 Neurostimulator implants in my spinal cord powered by two battery packs in my lower back. I am dependent upon several narcotics and one of them causes me to suffer short-term memory loss. I must take an amphetamine to make my body function every morning, and I wear Lidoderm (a form of Novocain) patches on my legs and back to help with the pain when I stand to teach.

I only tell you this to share with you an important lesson, and one that seemed to take me a while to accept as true. There is one thing I can assure you – self-pity has *never* helped me accomplish anything. It does me no good to feel sorry for myself or have others feeling sympathy for me – it is nothing but a waste of precious time.

It also does no good to feel sorry for ourselves when we have to teach a topic that we do not enjoy. Complaining and disdain will not help our law enforcers or recruits learn how to survive. Take it from a master of self-pity – when you find yourself in that state of mind, look for the nearest exit.

It really is true: You learn what is important in your life when you are about to lose it. I wish I would have had my current perspective on life twenty-five years ago. My priorities would have included hope, faith, and serving others much sooner, and I would have ensured that my God and my family would have never taken a back seat to anything.

"Self-pity is our worst enemy and if we yield to it, we can never do anything wise in this world." ~Helen Keller

How I Wrote This Book

I am not a writer – hopefully that has not been painfully obvious up to this point - but I knew it was my duty to write *Police Instructor*. I was asked by an academy commander if I would share my techniques, activities, and ideas with the other instructors. I agreed, and started by surveying hundreds of cadets and trainers to find out what their most common complaints and challenges were; I tried to find answers for each one. I continued past the complaints and began to include other methods of education and training from a variety of professions and groups. That variety is the foundation of *Police Instructor*.

I began to develop a handbook that would benefit instructors throughout Ohio, and then I began adding resources, information, and activities to benefit instructors across our nation. While researching, I made dozens of connections with police officers from other countries, and I asked them for their analysis and input on the guide. They not only added ideas but requested more of my materials as well as the book when it was completed. That is how the handbook grew from a simple handout for fellow instructors into a comprehensive resource for policing.

To prepare, I read several books on *how* to write non-fiction. *On Writing Well* by William Zinsser was my biggest help. I listened to his audio book a dozen times while driving back and forth to the academies and followed the advice and tips he gave. After applying his rules, I reduced the original manuscript by half.

On top of the photos and images found throughout the book, I decided to add some character by creating *SPIM (Super Police Instructor Man)*. I purchased a guide on cartooning, and with Gloria's help, spawned the cartoon characters leading you through the chapters. I wanted a book with unique characters since we serve a profession that is filled with unique people. I added a *SPIM Factoid* at the end of each chapter to ensure you smile while reading the book. I enjoyed writing the book (most of the time), and I want you to enjoy reading it.

Publishing the book at a reasonable cost for instructors proved to be harder than I originally thought it would be. One publisher wanted a *politically correct* version of the book to hit the shelves at nearly one hundred dollars. Another publisher wanted to split the book into two volumes and sell each for forty five dollars; both wanted to charge a fee to join the website. At those prices, the book would have collected dust while sitting on a shelf at an academy, university, or police agency – where it would not benefit anyone. *Police Instructor* must be in the hands of a trainer to be an effective resource for law enforcement training.

I have nothing against these publishers, but I decided to fulfill my mission through non-traditional methods to lower the cost. It required far more work and a family effort, but you can see the end result. It was finally published under our conditions and specifically for law enforcement and criminal justice educators.

The book also took *much* longer to finish than I had anticipated. I spent several years testing the techniques and activities with a variety of law enforcement audiences. I consumed over 40 books on public speaking, training techniques, group facilitation, active teaching methods, and slide design. I spent three months, before my last spinal implant surgery, getting all my notes and materials together into something that resembled a file system. After the surgery, I spent the next six months writing and rewriting the book – much more on rewriting.

I worked between 6 and 12 hours each day on the book, and when I finally had everything I wanted inside, it was nearly 500 pages. My time was then spent cutting out the fluff and repetitive material to make it as concise as I could. I have invested over 1600 hours in crafting the book and the website over the last nine months. Charles Dickens wrote *A Christmas Carol* in two weeks so I am not planning to change careers anytime soon.

My friend Nancy Neal, along with my wife Gloria and my son Richard Jr. were instrumental in proofreading the book, but no one invested more time on the project than my daughter Nadia. Her dedication and hard work gave the book clarity and kept it from sounding like a farm boy from Ohio wrote a *how-to guide for cops that teach stuff*. She may have read through the manuscript more than I did and all while working toward a graduate degree.

If I can write a book that benefits police instructors, you can deliver dynamic presentations, create engaging slides, and increase active learning for your next audience. Share the information and techniques you find useful with other instructors, and help us with our mission to improve law enforcement training everywhere. It may sound like I am reaching for the stars – believing we can improve law enforcement training with a website and a book – but I also believe the world will be a better place to live if we are successful. I am actually reaching for a galaxy far, far, away, but I believe in the importance of our mission that earnestly.

"If at first an idea isn't absurd there is no hope for it."
~Albert Einstein

Not the Last Word

Police Instructor is not my attempt to speak the last word on law enforcement education and training. The techniques, methods, suggestions, and tips are **NOT** absolutes for you to follow. They are resources for you to use, change, or adapt how you see fit. I hope to stimulate ideas, stories, discussions, and positive action by law enforcement instructors, criminal justice educators, field training officers, supervisors, school resource officers, sheriffs, and chiefs. I hope the book serves you and your students well throughout your career and theirs. We should be pleased with our advancements in law enforcement training, but we should never be content.

"They must create the right environment and culture that fuels people and their performance. Culture drives behavior, behavior drives habits, and habits create the future." ~Jon Gordon

SPIM Factoid

Google could calculate data as quickly as SPIM - if he were to sleep. He chooses not to.

Phalanx Law Enforcement

"A belief is something you will argue about. A conviction is something you will die for!" ~Howard Hendricks

The Phalanx is a formation credited to the Spartans that we still use today in law enforcement for crowd control. The Spartan soldiers would stand shoulder to shoulder forming a strong foundation that could withstand a formidable attack. Each soldier was responsible for the safety of their comrades on either side. Their shield protected the soldier on their left and their spear protected the soldier on their right. They may have used the same cliché' that we do, *"I've got your back."*

Phalanx LE is the *Richipedia* take on the values that were handed down by the Spartans that lived and died inside the formation. As instructors, we should be willing to stand shoulder to shoulder in our common cause – to train the finest guardians possible. By aiding those instructors around us, we build a strong foundation of knowledge that develops into wisdom for our students. They will stand strong against evil because of our guidance and example as a police instructor. *Phalanx LE* represents a foundation of integrity that will serve as a model for law enforcers around the world to follow.

> *"If one falls, the other can help his friend get up. But how tragic it is for the one who is all alone when he falls. There is no one to help him get up." ~Ecclesiastes 4:10*

Form A Phalanx Where You Serve

Society has placed the highest expectations possible on the police instructor, and from experience, I understand the pressures that come with training law enforcers. At times there is little available through training or resources to assist instructors. Most trainers receive eighty hours (or less) of instructor skills training and are expected to have the same results as a college professor. By networking with other like minded trainers, we can make up for the deficiencies we sometimes struggle with.

> Society has placed the highest expectations possible on the police instructor.

Build a foundation of knowledge with a fellow instructor you know or with dozens of instructors from the police academy where you teach. Then connect to other academies throughout your state, the nation, and around the globe. Share the stories and examples that you use with your class and inspire other instructors to do the same. We should not hesitate to share our ideas with others who are serving the same cause.

> *"Never doubt that a small group of thoughtful, committed people can change the world. Indeed. It is the only thing that ever has." ~Margaret Mead*

Why Did You Become a Police Instructor?

We can get overwhelmed and caught up in the liabilities, learning theories, and complex world of law enforcement training. We can forget why we first decided to share our wisdom and experience with others. Instructors are earnest about policing, and we care about the society our children will inherit.

I am a firm believer that only a guardian can train and fully prepare another guardian. This generation of instructors can do better than our predecessors did – all of society is counting on us.

Why is it that you are an instructor? What is your passion? How can you transfer your experience and wisdom to others? Why do you care about your students?

Police instructors have the power to make a crucial upgrade for law enforcement – one cop or cadet at a time. Each instructor impacts the lives of countless law enforcers who in-turn influence many others throughout their careers. What greater calling is there? Not many come to mind, but I am a little biased.

"If you cannot answer a man's argument, all is not lost; you can still call him vile names." ~ Elbert Hubbard

Instructors Hold Liberty in Their Hands

We are not teaching an Avon representative how to sell lipstick. If they mess it up, the worst thing that can happen is they lose a sale or some lady has ugly lips. We are training people who have the power to take away the *liberty* of others. The very foundation of freedom that Americans have died to protect since our nation was born. Since 1775, an estimated 1.34 million Americans have died during our wars and another 1.5 million injured. With nearly 3 million casualties of war, we should have a great deal of pride and humility knowing that we are entrusted with the duty to protect that freedom.

Life, liberty, and the pursuit of happiness must be upheld each day in America by law enforcers. Those you train now will hold the freedoms enjoyed by you and your family in their hands tomorrow. Is it not important to make every effort to train them well?

"I am only one, but still I am one. I cannot do everything, but still I can do something; and because I cannot do everything, I will not refuse to do something that I can do."
~Helen Keller

Forget the Pessimists

Don't let the pessimistic naysayers get you down. They will always exist on the fringe of any struggle that requires selfless service, determination, or loyalty. They are not worthy of your company, and truth be told, they wish they could be just like you. The intestinal fortitude that is part of your character is something that they will never know.

Never apologize for being a law enforcement officer, and never feel that you have to. We are not perfect, but I can think of no better profession on earth. When things look their worst, we need each other the most.

"In VALOR there is HOPE" ~Tacitus

Instructors Must Have Passion

I am not the most dynamic, best educated, or charismatic instructor around, but I am considered a great instructor by my students. Why? Because I share the same trait that other great instructors have – passion. I believe in the noble profession of law enforcement and the devoted men and women that protect society from evil.

Without passion our training may fall on deaf ears; you cannot inspire others unless you are first inspired. An engaging presentation will go a long way to gaining attention, but only the police instructor can take the presentation to a dynamic level that compels a learner to act.

Be passionate in discovering new methods to train law enforcers. By changing your perspective, you expand your possibilities to see something you were unable to see before. New ideas and unique insights will come from such a change, and they will benefit your students, your training, and your community.

I want to challenge you to be a producer of knowledge for fellow instructors – not just a consumer. Creativity does not happen by accident; you must intentionally pursue unique and innovative methods to enhance your craft. Combine your creativity and passion to write a better book than *Police Instructor* or design a more engaging website than *LEOtrainer.com*. Show your passion for training and join our mission to build a strong *Phalanx* – law enforcement style.

> **I want to challenge you to be a producer of knowledge for fellow instructors – not just a consumer.**

"It is not the critic who counts: not the man who points out how the strong man stumbles or where the doer of deeds could have done better. The credit belongs to the man who is actually in the arena, whose face is marred by dust and sweat and blood, who strives valiantly, who errs and comes up short again and again, because there is no effort without error or shortcoming, but who knows the great enthusiasms, the great devotions, who spends himself for a worthy cause; who, at the best, knows, in the end, the triumph of high achievement, and who, at the worst, if he fails, at least he fails while daring greatly, so that his place shall never be with those cold and timid souls who knew neither victory nor defeat." ~Theodore Roosevelt

Active Learning Index

Throughout the book you have read about innovative techniques to use for training law enforcers and cadets. They can help you create a positive experience for students while increasing retention and understanding. Variety is the key to effective training and the *Active Learning Index* will aid you in discovering it. Continually add to the index with your ideas, quotes, exercises, scenarios, and stories.

Look for opportunities to incorporate the techniques from this book as well as other sources into your presentation. If you only have a short amount of time, pick a controversial statement, inspirational quote, or a quick opening exercise. There is always enough time to add a unique point to the mix and start your class off with interest instead of monotony.

Opening Exercises

These activities serve to get students acquainted with each other and actively involved with your topic. They can take time away from your original lesson plan, but their impact is well worth the investment. A good opening exercise is something like an appetizer – it gives students a taste of what is to come and sets an engaging atmosphere early on.

Each exercise could be used with multiple topics; I will leave it to you to decide how or when to use them.

The Lie Game

Each student must come up with a lie about themselves (or you can assign them one). They also must come up with two truths that will go with the lie. Each student then stands in front of the class and tells the two truths and one lie. The rest of the class can ask a few questions to see if they can tell which one is the lie. The cadet will try to bluff their way through the interview. The activity will help your students begin to learn how to detect deception through vocal responses and gestures.

[The offer of candy to anyone who makes it through undetected is a great incentive for them to try hard.]

Cadets learn to look for deceptive clues and ask pointed questions of suspects who are hiding information from them. If the activity is used at different times throughout the academy, you will see a noticeable difference in their questioning skills.

Misperception

Instruct students to take an 8 ½" X 11" piece of paper and hold it out in front of them [lead them through with your own sheet of paper]. Have the students close their eyes during the rest of the exercise and provide them with the following instructions.

1. Fold your sheet of paper in half. Now tear off the upper right-hand corner.
2. Fold the paper in half again. This time tear off the upper left-hand corner.

3. Fold it in half one final time and tear off the lower right hand corner.

Allow the students to open their eyes when everyone is finished. Hold up your sheet and ask if they listened well comparing your paper to theirs. Of course, none will exactly match and some will have major differences. Ask them if you did a good job of communicating the task. Walk around and hold each student's sheet up next to yours for comparison. There is usually some laughter involved with each comparison.

Ask: "Why does your paper not match mine?" Listen for statements like, "You didn't let us ask questions" or "You weren't specific enough." Talk about how people can perceive what we say differently than our intended meaning, and how we do the same with them. As law enforcers, they must understand exactly what a victim, witness, or suspect is trying to tell them. They must confirm the details of what is seen and heard by any means possible.

Guess Which Square

This exercise serves as a quick opener to get cadets thinking through a problem instead of rushing to an answer. I do not know where the activity originated from, but it works well with several of our topics.

Display a grid containing 64 squares on the screen or white board. Select one square and write down the corresponding letter and number on an index card. Tell the students their job is to guess which square you chose. Do not allow them to talk with each other, and call on them one at a time allowing *yes* or *no* questions. Once they pass up 10 guesses stop them. Tell them that you are going to choose a new number and start over again, but this time let them take a minute and discuss their strategy as a group.

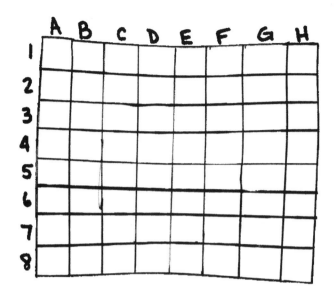

Most groups can guess the right square with only six questions once they think about it logically. They can ask you one question and reduce the squares by 50% each time. Their question should be something like, "Is your square in rows A through D?" Whether you answer *yes* or *no*, they just cut the possibilities in half. Their next question should be, "Is your square in rows 1 through 4?" If they continue cutting the possibilities by 50% with each question, they will have your square pinpointed with only six questions.

The object of the activity is to get the class working as a group and thinking problems through before jumping to an answer. The same qualities are important for law enforcers to have on the street. When there is time, we want them to think problems through and ask for the advice of others to find the most effective answer. Listening to a lecture without any interaction can never build these skills.

The activity works well with several topics. Community Policing: Use problem solving instead of just throwing a bunch of cops at the issue. Crime Scene Search: Plan your approach before rushing in and messing up the scene. Interview & Interrogation: Your questions need to be thought out and concise. Asking a suspect the wrong question can bring an interrogation to an abrupt halt.

Predictions & Profiling

Create groups of 4 to 6 students and give them the following instructions.

Your job is to predict how each person in your group will answer the following questions. Try to be specific and make bold guesses. When the predictions are finished have the person answer each of the questions and see if anyone guessed right. [You can have them keep score to add competition]

* Where did you grow up?
* What were you like in high school?
* What kind of music do you like?
* Were your parents strict or lenient?
* What are your hobbies?
* How many hours do you sleep at night?

Use the exercise as an introduction to the misconceptions of profiling and ask the following questions.

* Can we effectively profile someone we do not know just by the color of their skin, the way they dress, or ethnic heritage?
* Were you able to successfully profile your classmates?
* What information would you want to have before profiling someone involved in criminal activity?
* What information would you want another officer to have before they profiled someone you love?

It is a quick and effective opener for the debates involved with profiling. Then move through improperly profiling someone based on race, religion, or ethnic heritage. Proceed into proper criminal profiling methods that are ethical and accepted by the courts.

Toothpick Triangle

Give each cadet six toothpicks with the following challenge. I want you to create four triangles on your table with the six toothpicks I have provided you. They should be the same size.

Most will become frustrated in less than one minute. Ask them what they need to complete the task. They will want more toothpicks, but tell them they have all they need to complete the challenge. If no one figures out how to make four triangles after a few minutes, show them how to do it.

It is relatively easy if you make a three dimensional pyramid. You must start by making one triangle on the table using three toothpicks. Use the remaining three toothpicks to form a three dimensional pyramid above it. That makes four triangles on the table. Law enforcers need to think about problems in different ways and cannot rely on one problem solving method for every call they answer. If one solution does not work, they cannot just give up on a victim. They must look for another solution even if they become frustrated with the problem. We want them to become three dimensional law enforcers.

Letter of Regret

Have cadets write a letter to their loved ones. In the letter they must apologize for not putting enough effort into learning the necessary survival skills and for not taking their academy training seriously. Have them list the topics and areas you have covered to this point in the letter. Ask them to indicate next to each area if they dozed off, were thinking about other things, or playing with their cell phone. Ask them "How might that effect your survivability later?" Just writing the letter is emotional for some cadets and makes them realize there are consequences when you fail to train.

Use the letter as a challenge throughout the remainder of their training. For example: Point out that knowing the proper ways to spot a batterer and handle a domestic violence call can save their life. Point back to the letters they wrote and tell them "If you take this information for granted, your letters may be delivered sooner than you think." Ask: "How do you think your family will feel when the letter is delivered to them?" and "What do you need to do to make sure it never gets delivered?"

Collect the letters and record some of their responses. They can be eye opening for students and instructors alike. Give the letters back toward the end of the academy and challenge them to do everything possible to keep their letter from ever being delivered.

John Wayne Syndrome

Recruits come into the field of law enforcement with many different perceptions (mostly incorrect). Some believe they will ride out and handle everything single handedly like John Wayne, while others think they will have back-up on every call.

This is a quick exercise to discuss the misconceptions about law enforcement. Start with an image of John Wayne on the screen and ask them what made his characters so macho. You will get a flurry of manly answers.

Have cadets form a line standing shoulder to shoulder facing you. If they are the type of person who faces problems alone, have them go to the right side of the line. If they usually seek help from others in dealing with problems, they should go to the left side. Let the students work together to form a new single file line and determine what position each one should take.

Once they finish positioning themselves, talk to the cadets at each end. Ask them why they belong in those positions. Interview several other cadets throughout the line to find out why they chose the spots they are in. You will find contrasting viewpoints from one end to the other.

Explain how a law enforcement officer needs to combine the strengths found at both ends of the line. They must have the confidence to stand on their own and make important decisions. In contrast, they must be willing to take advice from other officers, as well as citizens, to carry out their duties.

People may point to the John Wayne type of cop as macho and refer to him as a Lone Ranger, but I like to remind them that even The Lone Ranger had back-up – Tonto.

Cadets will need to accept criticism and learn from others throughout their careers. In the academy, they will receive support and feedback from instructors and commanders. Once on a department, they will continue training with an FTO who will provide constant oversight, and when ready, they will be *cut loose* – but not *cut off.*

Once on their own, a rookie must learn how to determine when to act alone and when to involve others. Both are equally important to a successful career in policing.

Experiential Activities

Experiential learning activities are designed to bring meaning for your students from a direct experience with your lesson. Our audience of law enforcers and cadets learns best by *doing*, and any activity that provides them with interaction will help them understand more effectively.

At a Second Glance

I created this exercise to help cadets focus on deep issues that can be hidden from sight when they initially respond to a call, and realize things are not always what they appear to be.

Start by making groups of 4 to 6 students and give them the following list of people to rank. Number 1 will be the person they find the most reprehensible, and 5 should be the least offensive. Give the groups 10 minutes to discuss the individuals and rank each one.

* A woman leaves her 3 year old daughter home alone while she prostitutes herself.
* A 23 year old Heroin addict.
* A 20 year old who sells a joint to a neighbor.
* A 16 year old who shot a man in the back.
* A man who committed a sexual assault against a 15 year old girl.

Have each team explain how they determined who was the worst, and their justification for each of the rankings. After the groups have all presented their lists, show them the list again – *At a Second Glance.*

* A woman leaves her 3 year old daughter home alone while she prostitutes herself for $10. *She has lost her job and her husband ran out on her. Her child will slowly starve without the money. She has never been forced to do anything illegal before in her entire life.*
* A 23 year old Heroin addict. *The young man served 3 tours in Afghanistan where he saw several friends killed by road side bombs. He was diagnosed with PTSD but was too ashamed to take help from the VA Hospital.*

✻ A 20 year old who sells a joint to a neighbor. *The neighbor is an 11 year old. The dealer knows the boy's father is an alcoholic, making the 6ᵗʰ grader an easy target.*

✻ A 16 year old who shot a man in the back. *The man was attempting to rape the boy's mother after breaking into their home.*

✻ A man who committed a sexual assault against a 15 year old girl. *The man is 18, and the victim is his 15 year old girlfriend. The sex was consensual, and the girl's parents do not care, but it is against the law in Ohio.*

Ask the class if they would like to keep their list in the same order with the new information they have just learned. Give them another 10 minutes to re-organize their choices.

Ask each group what changed from the first time they judged the group. The information was not false – just incomplete. Let them know the information will always be incomplete if they fail to ask the right questions and build rapport with people.

The activity does a good job of catching your audience off guard, and it gives them a small glimpse into the realities of police work – where things are always changing. I use real people from my encounters as a police officer in the activity so I can speak to questions, or beliefs, that arise from the exercise. For instance, I had a student in one class state that a whore is always a whore, and there was always another choice for the woman in the activity. I told the class the woman's story and admitted that I was of the same opinion as the cadet when I was a rookie.

The woman's husband had abandoned her and their daughter, and cleaned out the couple's bank account for good measure. They were hungry and living out of their car when I picked her up for soliciting prostitution. She pleaded with me, *"I am just trying to feed my kid."* With great disgust, I told her she could get food stamps. In fact she had applied for them, but there was a 3 week wait. Then I told her she should have gone to a soup kitchen or a homeless shelter. She began to weep as she explained *"We went to the soup kitchen but we were raped just outside the entrance."* She looked to her nine year old daughter who was also in tears at this point. I was done passing judgment on the lady and handing out advice for something I knew nothing about.

I grew up on a farm and went to work as a city cop. I had quite a learning curve and the woman taught me a lesson I would never forget. Our values are based on our personal knowledge, and until that day I was sure everyone like her was a whore. After that day I recognized her as a courageous parent willing to do whatever it took to feed her children. She taught me more than I could have ever taught her.

Those are the stories that can impact a cadet with a reality that no lecture ever can. Combined with experiential activities they are sure to gain the attention of your students and compel them to learn.

15 & Criminal

I created *15 & Criminal* to use with the *Juvenile Justice* topic, but it will also work well with: Ethics & Professionalism, Community Diversity, Community Policing, or Civil Liability & Use of Force.

Create two debate teams. One will argue for rehabilitation and release of the juvenile defendant. The other will serve as the prosecutor and argue why the juvenile should be incarcerated in a detention facility. Once the groups receive a scenario, give them a few minutes to prepare their opening arguments. Have one student from the prosecution start with a short opening, and then allow the other group to rebut the statement. Ensure a new student speaks on behalf of their group with each assignment. The remaining students should be feeding their representative information on what to say, based on their previous group discussions.

After the first scenario, switch the groups so they can debate from both sides of the system. Have them argue whether the juvenile should be incarcerated, receive counseling, attend boot camp, be placed in foster care, or released. What is the likelihood they will repeat the crime? What effect will it have on their family and the victim? Will placing them in jail with other criminals have a positive or negative outcome on the community?

* 15 year old girl steals her aunt's car and goes for a joy ride with her best friend. She crashes the car but no one is injured. She has no criminal record and the aunt's insurance is paying for the damages. The juvenile is remorseful for her actions, and her aunt does not want any type of action taken against her niece.

* 15 year old boy steals his neighbor's bicycle that is valued at $1,200.00. He has stolen once before but was cooperative with the officers.

* 15 year old female gang banger broke into a local convenience store to steal food and cash. She has a criminal record for theft and vandalism, and she resisted arrest.

* 15 year old boy hit his mother in the face when she took away his Xbox. Her lip was bloody but there were no serious injuries. He has no criminal record but has been disciplined multiple times at school for disorderly behavior. He assaulted the arresting officer, but his mother pleads for leniency.

* 15 year old boy molested his 4 year old niece. There was suspicion that he was molested as a child as well, but the investigation was unfounded. He is uncooperative with the police and states they never helped him when he needed it. The niece's parents want the boy to go to prison forever. She was traumatized by the experience and required psychological help.

Students will find that there are two sides to these types of cases. There are reasons for, and against, all facets of the juvenile justice system. As you listen to the debate you will hear a variety of discussions and points of view. Use what you hear to formulate questions for the class discussion to follow.

Ask your students which case was the hardest to argue, for or against. One final question for the class: "If this was your 15 year old child would you want them to have the punishment you gave the others?" The students who have their own children will usually have a different reply than those who do not. It makes for a great conversation about the juvenile justice system, and that is what we are after.

Students will understand these dilemmas better when they debate them. The cases are real as are the suspects, victims, and families. Let the students know these are the types of calls law enforcers deal with every day. Juvenile crime represents a high percentage of police calls regardless of where they will work, and being cynical will not help them.

WMD (Weapons of Mass Decisions)

This activity can be as involved for your audience as *Neil Island.* I designed *WMD* for the *Community Diversity* topic, but it will also work well with: *Ethics & Professionalism, Community Policing,* and *Role of the Peace Officer.*

A full-scale exchange of WMD has just occurred and you are among the 15 people who are left on earth. You have made it to a survival bunker, but you soon find there are only enough resources for 9 people to survive inside. You must decide who stays to carry on the American Dream, and who must be sacrificed. The group consists of the following:

* ☆ You are a 42-year-old white male police officer in full gear. Your wife who is a Christian missionary is with you. She is also white and 42.
* ☆ A 35-year-old nuclear physicist, male, Muslim, and single.
* ☆ A 34-year-old mother who is on probation for child abuse, and her 14-year-old son.
* ☆ A 42-year-old psychologist, female, Indian, and single.
* ☆ A couple, both are 21-years-old and college students. One is studying history and the other chemistry. Both are male, one is Asian and the other one is white.
* ☆ A 26-year-old truck driver, male, black, and Muslim. His wife is a 25-year-old, white, stay at home mom. They have their children with them. Three girls 2, 5, and 7-years-old.
* ☆ A 58-year-old preacher, black, Pentecostal, male, and single.
* ☆ A 19-year-old American soldier who is an Egyptian immigrant and disabled from a previous combat tour.

Divide the class into small groups of 3 to 5 students. Display the exercise on a slide or provide it to your class in a handout. Allow 20 to 30 minutes for the groups to discuss who they will keep and who they will leave out to die.

Move around and listen to their conversations and develop follow up questions. Have each group identify who they kept, and for what reason. Then have each group give their reasons for those who were left out to perish. Instruct them to stand in front of the class as a group and deliver their decisions together. Have them identify what disagreements their group had.

What were the major reasons they cited for leaving people out? Probe for stereotyping, but assure them that we all have different types of bias in our lives and honesty is what you are looking for. Most groups will keep the police officer since that is their role in the exercise – who wants to leave their self out? Should the officer volunteer to be a sacrifice? Is that not a decision police officers must face every day? What about his missionary wife? Would she volunteer as well? If any families were separated ask them why? If a family is the American dream, should we so readily split one up?

I did not design the activity to have right or wrong answers. The intent is to stimulate conversations that help students to examine their own beliefs and biases. It will also help each member see how others differ in opinion.

Will they be able to serve all citizens within their community regardless of their ethnic heritage, religious belief, or sexual orientation? What if the cost of that service is their very life? That is the oath they are required to take to represent law enforcement.

Richville **Crime Prevention**

This activity was created to compliment the *Community Policing* and *Crime Prevention* topics. It will help cadets to recognize how people and communities are affected by different types of crime. The activity will help them find creative and innovative ways to solve the problems that arise.

Start by making several groups of 4 to 6 students with the responsibility to solve neighborhood disorders. Instruct each group to write down their plan on how to deal with the problem faced by their community. After giving them enough time to come up with a list, allow each group to explain their plan of action for solving each issue. After each team has presented their ideas allow them to debate which plan will work best to solve the problem. Only give them one problem to solve at a time or give each group a different problem all together (depending on the available time).

* Dozens of citizens are complaining of loud car stereos at all hours of the day and night in one suburban neighborhood. You have received several vehicle descriptions and one license plate from reported complaints.

* The residents of a small farm town have been burglarized a dozen times over the past month. The same M.O. has been used in which a suspect knocks on the front door and if no one answers they go to the back and break in through a window. The few times a resident has answered their door a male white in his 20's has asked for directions and claimed to be lost. One citizen believed he was riding a bicycle.

* An urban neighborhood has a speeding problem. While the speed limit is only 25 through this part of town dozens of citizens claim that multiple people are driving through at high rates of speed. Some claim the speeders routinely go 50 and 60 mph, and there are hundreds of young children living in the neighborhood. With a limited amount of green space, they commonly play on the sidewalks and in the street where they are in danger.

* A popular city park is being vandalized with graffiti and damage to the buildings. Citizens are now using the park less and less with the profanity sprayed about where children can see it. The graffiti seems to be gang related with symbols from the *Folk* and *People Nations* present.

* One suburban neighborhood has several foreclosed homes that are now vacant. Teens and young adults started vandalizing the empty houses by breaking out windows but

have now turned them into make shift clubhouses. Teens are now using alcohol and drugs inside the houses, and a 13 year old girl was sexually assaulted at one location.

* A local hotel is reported to have *call girl* services running out of several rooms. Several guests reported the apparent prostitution operation and described the suspects. They indicated at least two of the prostitutes they observed appeared to be girls in their early teens.

After the groups have provided their solution to each problem, give them one final assignment. Have them rank the problems from the one they feel deserves to be given the highest priority, to the problem that can wait to be dealt with. Then, have them answer the following questions.

* Why is this problem ranked higher than those below it?
* What risks are created for the community by this problem?
* What manpower and financial issues must be considered?

Allow each group to list their findings on the board for everyone to see. Have them present their reasons and the risks they identified. You will be surprised by the creativity shown by some groups in solving problems. Use follow up questions, or a group discussion, based on what you hear.

* What do you tell the citizens from the other neighborhoods who have to wait for a response?
* What can go wrong if we wait to respond to any one of these issues?
* What should you do if your response does not work?

Richville reveals problems and risks associated with acts that are considered minor by some. Speeding does not seem like a big deal until a person is driving recklessly through a neighborhood filled with kids. Likewise, some may not think prostitution affects anyone outside of the business until they hear a minor is being forced to participate. Cadets begin to realize how important their crime prevention role will be for the communities they serve.

Instant Aging

This is a great activity for *Community Diversity* or *Victim's Rights.* It shows young cadets what it means to deal with an aging body. Randomly choose several cadets for the activity. Place cotton in their ears, latex gloves on their hands, marbles or rocks in their shoes, and have them wear extra thick (cheap dollar store) reading glasses. Require them to walk around the classroom and then watch a short video showing a crime in progress. Instruct them to write a summary of what they saw and heard with the new restrictions applied to their bodies. They will see how disabilities, that might seem minor to others, can quickly add up to inhibit a person's senses. The restrictions can prevent the identification of a suspect making the elderly victim an easy target.

This type of exercise can have a tremendous impact on a cadet's understanding of the disabled population who are counting on law enforcers to protect and serve them.

LEO Game of Life

This game is used to show what can happen if people truly work together for the good of everyone.

Have the cadets form six groups of any size. Show the class the combinations board below and tell each group to discuss and then choose P or S by writing the letter down on a piece of paper (You can label these Police and Sheriff for more competition). Repeat this 5 times and then record the scores for each group.

Combinations	Points Awarded
All choose P	All lose 2 points
Five P; One S	Ps win 2; S loses 10
Four P; Two S	Ps win 4; Ss lose 8
Three P; Three S	Ps win 6; Ss lose 6
Two P; Four S	Ps win 8; Ss lose 4
One P; Five S	P wins 10; Ss lose 2
All choose S	All win 2 points

After the first two rounds, you may choose to allow teams to negotiate with each other. Teams will be trying to figure out how to win while making the other groups lose.

After the game is over, you will see a variety of reactions from your Type A cadets. Some will be upset with others who did not work together, and those who lost may act like victims. The teams have the power to make sure that everyone wins, but it rarely happens. After discussing the reactions you witnessed during the game, point out some simple truths.

The actions of one team invariably affected the others. In the same way, the self-centered actions of one officer can have a negative impact on an entire department. While officers should maintain their individualism, they should always realize that they represent something much larger than themselves.

The other important point to make is that people with power do not always want to negotiate with others. They don't feel the need to worry about others who cannot benefit them in some way, but officers who wield power must be able to work with everyone involved. An officer can end up seeing law enforcement as a competition, but it should never be that way; the stakes are too high.

Field Observation

With the required hours in the classroom, it may be impossible to take your class on a field trip, but they still need some real world experience. We teach adults in the police academy that they do not require a chaperone to visit law enforcement related sites.

The following assignments are only suggestions for you to use. You may decide to allow your students to choose their own assignment from a list you provide. Regardless of the assignment, make sure the cadets take some notes that they can share with the class.

☆ Ride along with a different law enforcement agency each month of the academy. Consider a mix of agencies including villages, large cities, counties, state, and federal. Try to have students assigned to other units as well: detective section, crime scene investigation, school resource officer, crime prevention, etc.

★ Attend a criminal or traffic court hearing. Mayor's courts are held in the evening hours if cadets cannot attend court during business hours.

★ Visit a juvenile detention center or a children services agency.

★ Attend a neighborhood watch meeting, visit a homeless shelter, or work at a soup kitchen.

★ Request police records from a local agency and bring them to class the following day. Require them to obtain different types of records: accident report, crime scene photographs, domestic violence report, traffic citation, etc. Let them experience the public records system first hand.

When students complete their assignments have them share the experience with the class the following day. It provides a variety of experiences that will be shared by everyone throughout the academy. Ask students:

★ How were you treated by the person you shadowed? Were they open and honest or conceited and rude?

★ Was the experience a good one?

★ What did you learn that you did not know before?

★ Would you have handled it differently if you were the LEO?

Homework

Consider different types of assignments for your cadets to complete after classroom hours that will help them continue to gain knowledge on your topic.

★ If you are teaching the topic on *Use of Force,* assign students different Supreme Court rulings affecting the way they must apply force as an officer. When they return the following day, have the students form *Tactical Training Squads* and teach each other what they learned during their research. Let them instruct each other as they combine the individual court rulings together into a common understanding of the law.

* Assign each cadet with the name of a law enforcement officer who was killed in action. Require the student to research the officer's personal life and the circumstances around their death. Have a different cadet report on an *Officer Down* each day throughout the academy. Encourage them to report on the family that was left behind as well as the suspect's information and the final outcome.

Participation Activities

Start – Stop – Continue - Change

At the beginning of your lesson have students write four words on their handout: Start-Stop-Continue-Change. After your training is completed, have the class return to the list. Ask them to consider what they have learned and how it can benefit them as officers. Instruct them to answer the following questions:

* ☆ What should you **Start** doing?
* ☆ What should you **Stop** doing?
* ☆ What should you **Continue** doing?
* ☆ What should you **Change**?

This simple technique is used by trainers in the business world to help their audience focus on what they have learned and what to do with it when they get back to work. It can be equally as effective with any law enforcement audience you train.

Judge and Jury

Judge and Jury is a group exercise used to present scenarios to students that will require some deliberation and thought. I use it primarily with the *Legal and Ethics* topics, but it will work in other areas as well. Place the students into juries of four to eight members. Pose a situation through a scenario or relevant police video. Give them four or five choices – or you may choose to leave the sentencing entirely up to them.

Judge and Jury can place students in the position of civilians judging the actions of law enforcement officers. With a topic like *Use of Force,* show a video of an officer repeatedly hitting a suspect. Students (the jury) must look at the evidence and decide if the force used was reasonable based on decisions like *Graham v. Connor (1985).* If not, they must decide if there was a civil rights violation under *42 U.S.C;* and determine if criminal charges are appropriate.

Judge and Jury is more than just an interactive review; it serves as a sobering reality that your students will also be judged for their actions, and it gives them one more reason to be attentive in class.

When each group has reached their verdict, have them read it to the others. You can facilitate a class discussion on the topic and have each jury explain their decision and what behavior made them rule that way.

Media Relations

Have the class watch a variety of police related videos that illustrate different scenarios they will encounter. Have cadets individually write out a media release for one of the events they just observed. Instruct them to write down possible questions that reporters may ask them once the release is made and what they feel the correct responses are.

Form small groups and have each team work to create a final media release for each event. Set a time limit and have each group give their media release to the rest of the class. Then allow the other students to pose questions commonly asked by journalists and see how they respond under pressure.

Crisis Interview

Use this method when teaching good questioning skills with victims or witnesses immediately after a crime.

Pick a video of a convenience store robbery with several suspects committing the crime, but consider the crime from the victim's viewpoint. Before playing the video for the class begin by role-playing the part of the store clerk in the video. Have the cadets ask you interview questions to prepare a police report and further investigate the crime. Give them short responses and only provide the information they requested. Write their questions down on the flip chart along with your responses. Then play the actual video of the crime.

After watching the video, ask if their questions would have stimulated good answers from the victim. Did they ask open ended questions that would encourage a victim to tell a story? Would all the relevant details be uncovered by the questions they asked? Should they have asked questions a different way?

Explain that small details that seem unimportant to victims can actually be the information we need to solve a crime.

Consider using videos of purse snatchings, shopliftings, and assaults. There are multiple videos of criminal activity available at LEOtrainer.com/crimes. Also search for relevant videos on websites like YouTube and local news sites. The method helps you make a powerful point that your students will not soon forget.

Controversial or Peculiar

Consider any well known book, article, news story, or quote as a unique way to start your next class. I purposely use controversial statements that I know will make a class of cops or cadets mad. If they are mad, they are listening. They want to know why I used it and what comes next. Do not be afraid to challenge their core beliefs or yours – they will come out stronger and be more attentive knowing that nothing is off limits in your presentation.

I usually place short statements on the screen for students to ponder and then follow up with the remainder of the information.

PTSD & Stress

True or False: As many as one third of law enforcers in this country are impaired by PTSD (Post Traumatic Stress Disorder) and cannot function well, if at all. ~from the book CopShock by Allen R. Kates

The statement is true and backed up by several different studies. Here are a few follow up statistics to drive the point home for your audience of veterans or cadets.

* Rates of PTSD among American police officers are as high as 35% (Mann & Neece, 1990).

* Law enforcement personnel have been reported to have three times the rate of suicide, increased alcohol use and cardiovascular diseases, and twice the rate of divorce compared to the general population (Marmar et al., 2007; McCaslin et al., 2007).

* 69% of law enforcement officers who retired early left for psychological reasons (Miller, 1996).

Rookie Stress

True or False: Over 50% of rookie officers will encounter a critical incident in their first year?

* It's false. It is much higher with 94.5% of police recruits reporting exposure to at least one critical incident during their first year of police service (Marmar et al., 2007).

The Costs of Police Work

True or False: Departments send you through polygraph examinations, background checks, and psychological tests because law enforcers are expensive to retain. The cost to train an officer can average $50,000. The yearly expense of that same officer averages another $60,000?

* False: Retention of personnel is critical to the success of a police department. It costs as much as $500,000 to train and $93,300 per year to employ just one officer (Dept. of Justice, Bureau of Justice Statistics).

We Need Warriors

Ask your cadets the following question. *"Can we survive without doctors and hospitals?"*

I always get a quick answer back from my class, *"Of course not."* They answer without thinking about our ancestors who survived for the past 10,000 years without medical sciences (but with 4 spinal implants I'm happy we have them now). After allowing the class time to debate the topic, place the following statement from *On Combat* (Lt. Colonel Dave Grossman and Loren W. Christensen) on the screen, and ask the students if the statement is true.

* We could go for a generation without the doctors... but civilization would continue. If, however, we went but a single generation without the warriors who are willing to confront human aggression every day, then within the span of that generation we would truly be "both damned and doomed."

It will start a great discussion and help our future guardians see the importance of warriors in our culture.

Crapping Your Pants

Is it natural to wet your pants when you are in a life and death situation? Should we let officers know what physical and biological changes they may encounter in such circumstances?

* Research shows that if you have a "load" in your lower intestines during a highly stressful survival situation, it's going to go. Your body says, "Bladder Control? I don't think so. Sphincter control? We don't need no stinking sphincter control!" What do you do if that happens? You keep on fighting. ~On Combat, Lt. Col. Dave Grossman

Tunnel Vision

Out of 10 *officer involved* shootings, how many police officers would suffer from tunnel vision?
* Eight out of 10 suffered tunnel vision. ~ Alexis Artwohl, Ph.D. is an internationally recognized behavioral science consultant to law enforcement, and she is an advisory board member for the Force Science Research Institute.

Killing Ain't Easy

In WWII only 15% to 20% of trained riflemen fired their weapons at exposed enemies when alone. If a leader ordered them to fire, nearly all did, but you won't have anyone commanding you. ~Study by General S.L.A. Marshal
* These figures have dramatically increased with realistic targets and training.
* As a cop or a peacekeeper, your job is not to kill, it is to serve and protect. To do that, you may have to kill. ~On Combat, Lt. Col. Grossman
* This is the great paradox of combat: If you are truly prepared to kill someone, you are less likely to have to do it. ~On Combat, Lt. Col. Grossman

Cop Dreams

You are about to be killed, but your gun will not fire. You do not have enough strength to pull the trigger or the bullets just dribble out the end. Can you imagine such a dream coming from a macho cop?
* These are called performance anxiety dreams and are common among law enforcers. Training has been found to

be the best way to subdue the dreams. Some officers will stop having the dreams just by finding out they are common in law enforcement. Let them know.

Racism

"We don't know how much racism was involved" says Jerome H. Skolnick, a law professor at the University of California, Berkeley, "but I believe that racist police are more likely to be brutal and brutal police are more likely to be racist." When black people see a police car in Los Angeles, says state assemblyman Curtis Tucker, "they don't know whether justice will be meted out or whether judge, jury and executioner is pulling up."

Though nonwhites account for 60% of Los Angeles' polyglot population, white officers make up 61% of the L.A.P.D. Similar imbalances exist in many heavily ethnic communities around the U.S. and, says sociologist James Marquart of Sam Houston State University, this pattern can encourage police violence. "White police officers don't understand a lot of things that go on in these areas," says Marquart. "One way to deal with that is to use force. It goes across all cultural boundaries." [both paragraphs are from an article in Time Magazine, March 25, 1991 just after the Rodney King beating was shown to Americans for the first time. Title: Police Brutality!]

Create Skepticism: Sex Offender GPS

I can guarantee you that no registered predator will ever be able to hide from justice again, and we can now protect our children as well as adult victims from these people. They will no longer need to be tracked by probation or parole officers, and that will help communities during hard times. The death penalty is only allowed for premeditated murder, so that is not my solution. [The students will not only be skeptical, they will be interested in what comes next.] After the brief discussion, tell them the solution is implanting GPS chips in each offender. If they are registered, they get a chip. No choice. Is this okay with the class?

Many will say yes. Let them debate with other classmates who disagree.

There is another group to receive the chips. Police chiefs are demanding that all new officers receive the same chip so they can ensure that the officers serve with integrity and honesty. The chips will prevent officers from frequenting disreputable places and people deemed off limits by their agencies. Is this okay with the class? Would it serve society to track both groups in the same way?

Does Spirituality Help Law Enforcers?

Undisputed evidence of the wounds inflicted upon officers as the result of acute and chronic exposures during and after investigative activities, whether short or long, cry out for the development and implementation of safeguards. The cultivation of spirituality in law enforcement, at both the individual and organizational levels, can operate as an invisible weapon for wounded warriors. *"Once you choose law enforcement as a career you give up the right to be unfit. This must apply to fitness both mentally and physically."*

* Spirituality Enables Stress Management
* Spirituality Accelerates Performance
* Spirituality Enhances Practice
* Spirituality Governs Intuitive Policing
* Spirituality Governs Emotional Intelligence
* Spirituality Nurtures Ethics
* Spirituality Fosters Longevity

The FBI Law Enforcement Bulletin – January, 2009. Spirituality: An Invisible Weapon for Wounded Warriors. By Special Agent Samuel L. Feemster M.Div., J.D.

Quotes & Proverbs

Use a proverb or quote related to your topic to make a quick point, kick off your presentation, or start a group discussion. Asking students to react to a quote will create immediate involvement with your topic. I have included relevant quotes throughout *Police Instructor* and a few here in the *Active Learning Index*. There are also hundreds of Internet resources where you can find quotes on any topic. Use your imagination when you look for quotes or controversial statements, and don't be afraid to quote yourself. As you have seen, I do it all the time. If I don't quote myself, who will?

"The earth's atmosphere contains nitrogen, oxygen, and stupidity. After a career in law enforcement I have learned which has the most mass." ~Richipedia

"We will have to repent in this generation not merely for the hateful words and actions of the bad people, but for the appalling silence of the good people." ~Martin Luther King Jr.

"The world is a dangerous place to live, not because of those who do evil, but because of those who watch it and let it happen." ~Albert Einstein

"I feel very much like the mosquito who found himself unexpectedly in a nudist colony. I don't know where to begin." ~Senator Edmund Muskie

"Laziness will cause you pain." ~Vee Arnis Jitsu School

"When a naked man is chasing a woman through an alley with a butcher's knife and a hard-on, I figure he isn't out collecting for the Red Cross." ~Dirty Harry

"Don't look where you fall, but where you slipped." ~African Proverb

"Don't hit at all if it is honorably possible to avoid hitting; but never hit soft." ~Theodore Roosevelt

"I thought growing up was something that happened automatically as you got older. But it turns out it's something you have to choose to do." ~Scrubs

"Liberty may be endangered by the abuse of liberty, but also by the abuse of power." ~James Madison

"The essence of Government is power; and power, lodged as it must be in human hands, will ever be liable to abuse." ~James Madison

"What students would learn in American schools above all is the religion of Jesus Christ." ~George Washington

"All my life, I always wanted to be somebody. Now I see that I should have been more specific." ~Jane Wagner

'History doesn't repeat itself, but it rhymes." ~Mark Twain

"The ultimate measure of a man is not where he stands in moments of comfort and convenience, but where he stands at times of challenge and controversy." ~Dr. Martin L. King, Jr.

"A pessimist sees difficulty in every opportunity; an optimist sees the opportunity in every difficulty." ~Winston Churchill

"The individual who refuses to defend his rights when called by his government, deserves to be a slave, and must be punished as an enemy of his country and friend to her foe." ~Andrew Jackson

"If the rabble were lopped off at one end and the aristocrat at the other, all would be well with the country." ~Andrew Johnson

"We will bring the terrorists to justice; or we will bring justice to the terrorists. Either way, justice will be done." ~George W. Bush

Police Instructor © 2011

Infamous Case Examples

Use infamous cases that are relevant to your topic. This type of case can offer an interesting correlation that will engage cadets from the start. The following are just a sampling of cases you may decide to use, but there are many others that may share more relevance with your topic.

John Wayne Gacey: He was an American serial killer known as the "Killer Clown." He raped and murdered 33 teenage boys and young men between 1972 and 1978. Gacy buried 26 of his victims in the crawlspace of his home and three others elsewhere on his property, discarding the remaining four victims in a nearby river. He was able to disguise his behavior behind the persona of a businessman and community volunteer.

Gacy became known as the "Killer Clown" due to his charitable services at fundraising events, parades and children's parties where he would dress as "Pogo the Clown," a character he devised himself.

In 1975, Gacy was appointed director of Chicago's annual Polish Constitution Day Parade — an annual event he was to supervise from 1975 until 1978. Through his work with the parade, Gacy met and was photographed with then First Lady Rosalynn Carter.

Atlanta Child Murders: Would you think a conviction based solely on fibers and hairs is sufficient today to convict a suspect of murder? Even on death row? What about forensics technology from the 1970's? Would it be good enough to execute someone for murder? What if they are believed responsible for 26 murders involving children and young men?

Wayne Bertram Williams is an American serial killer who committed most of the Atlanta Child Murders that occurred from 1979 through 1981. In 1982 Williams was found guilty of two murders. After his conviction, the Atlanta police declared that an additional 23 of the 29 child murders were solved, with Williams shown to be the murderer. Fibers from clothing and carpet along with hairs from Williams' dog provided a strong circumstantial case.

Jon Benet Ramsey: In this case, the police department conducted a crime scene search after the parents found a ransom note, and their daughter missing from her room. The police somehow missed her body with the initial search, which was later discovered in the basement of the house – she had been strangled to death. Does this show they are incompetent? Or does it show cops are human, and simply make human mistakes? What might have caused them to miss the body with the initial search? How much evidence do you think you will miss in your career?

Jeffrey Dahmer: Dahmer murdered 17 men and boys between 1978 and 1991, with the majority of the murders occurring between 1987 and 1991. His murders were particularly gruesome, involving rape, dismemberment, necrophilia and cannibalism. On November 28, 1994, he was beaten to death by an inmate at the Columbia Correctional Institution, where he had been incarcerated.

When he was eight years old, he moved with his family to Bath, Ohio. Dahmer's early childhood was by all accounts normal, but he grew increasingly withdrawn and uncommunicative between the ages of 10 and 15, showing little interest in any hobbies or social interactions. He biked around his neighborhood looking for dead animals, which he dissected at home or in the woods nearby. In one instance, he went so far as to put a dog's head on a stake.

During his arrest an officer looked in the refrigerator and found a human head. Further searching of the apartment revealed three more severed heads, multiple photographs of murdered victims, and severed hands and penises. There were signs before the discovery was made that might have saved some of his victims.

On September 26, 1988, one day after moving into his Milwaukee apartment, he was arrested for drugging and sexually fondling a 13-year-old boy. He was sentenced to five years probation and one year in a work release camp. He was required to register as a sex offender. Shortly thereafter, he began a string of murders that ended with his arrest in 1991.

Bath School Disaster: A school bombing in Bath Township, Michigan, on May 18, 1927, killed 38 elementary school children, two teachers, four other adults and the bomber himself. Another 58 people were injured. Most of the victims were children in the second to sixth grades (7–12 years of age) attending the Bath Consolidated School. Their deaths constitute the deadliest act of mass murder in a school in U.S. history (not Columbine like many think). The perpetrator was school board member Andrew Kehoe, aged 55, who was upset by a property tax levied to fund the construction of the school building. He blamed the additional tax for financial hardships which led to foreclosure proceedings against his farm. These events apparently provoked Kehoe to plan his attack.

On the morning of May 18, Kehoe murdered his wife and set his farm buildings on fire. As fire fighters arrived at the farm, an explosion devastated the north wing of the school building. He used a detonator to ignite dynamite and hundreds of pounds of pyrotol which he had secretly planted inside the school over the course of many months. As rescuers started gathering at the school, Kehoe drove up, stopped, and detonated a bomb inside his shrapnel-filled vehicle, killing himself, the school superintendent, and several others. During the rescue efforts searchers discovered an additional 500 pounds of unexploded dynamite and pyrotol planted throughout the basement of the school's south wing.

Rapidly Evolving Scenarios

Law enforcers have to make quick decisions, and the average person has no idea what a *rapidly evolving* situation really looks like. Neither do cadets, but you can start clueing them in with some creative role-playing. The following interactive scenarios will grab their attention with situations that have actually occurred. Involving them in a rapidly evolving situation brings tension and emotion into the classroom. Consider using your own experiences, or stories you have heard, to illustrate what a rapidly evolving situation looks like.

Purse Snatcher

I first used this role-play when I was asked to teach a high school class about police work. I have used it many times since with topics like *Observation, Perception, & Description* or *Witness Misidentification* with academy cadets.

Begin lecturing the class on your topic. The best time to spring this on a cadet class is when they are copying one of the SPOs (Student Performance Objectives) into their notebooks. Have a personal item sitting close to you or in your hand. A wallet, a small bag, even the projector remote will do. Have a volunteer (not a cadet from the class or someone they have seen before) run into the class and push you aside. Have a shocked look on your face and make an appropriate comment for someone who has just suffered a strong arm robbery. They should grab the item and run out of the room. Have them wait in the hallway where they cannot be seen. Have the volunteer wear a hooded sweatshirt and gloves that will hide their features and race. Watch the reactions of your students for a lively discussion.

I have only had one student in the dozens of role plays ever run after the volunteer, and they had previous law enforcement experience. The rest just sit there in shock waiting for someone else to take action. Once you put their minds at ease, ask them to write down a description of the suspect in their notebooks. Then have them write down the appropriate charges for the crime. You can move right into a class discussion or have them form groups to compare their descriptions. There will be major disagreements on the color of clothing, race, age, and sex. Try to mislead them on the description, and see if they are easily persuaded.

Discuss the discrepancies between the students on the suspect's description and criminal charges. Then ask why no one went after the suspect. You will get a variety of answers and several egos may get bruised by the simple question. Reinforce the reality that they can no longer sit on the side lines and wait for others to act once they are sworn in as police officers. There can be no "I don't want to get involved" attitudes in law enforcement.

When you are ready, bring the volunteer back into the classroom so they can see him or her. Consider using a female volunteer whenever possible. I rarely have anyone identify her as anything but a male suspect. They make the assumption that crimes such as this are perpetrated only by men. Everyone misses descriptors of the suspect, and that helps them understand how hard it can be for a witness who was just involved in a critical incident to recall key information. The scenario covers a host of discussion topics for your academy class.

Pushing the Hair

Rub your hair from back to front several times without talking. The students may look a little puzzled, or even laugh. Ask if they were intimidated. They probably are not at this point, but tell them they should be ready to fight every time they see it on the street. It is a proven sign of aggression that has been researched and witnessed by law enforcement. Have them list other signs of aggression in a group. Videos of assaults are one method to show cadets how the signals may appear. Show several examples to your students or provide a short story of an incident in which you spotted the behavior and averted an attack.

The activity is not just an exercise for officer safety. Use it to point out how these signals could allow a frisk under *Terry v.*

Ohio by indicating that the person meets one of the criteria –
dangerous.

Spanish for Cops

This quick exercise works well with topics like *Gang
Awareness, Community Diversity, Foot Patrol,* and *Stops &
Approaches.* It only takes a few minutes to role-play, but it has a
lasting impact on any law enforcement class.

Pick a student to help you with the activity, and instruct them
to shake their head in agreement regardless of what you say. Pick
another student to act as an officer conducting an interview of
you and your new accomplice. Advise them that you and your
partner fit the profile of drug traffickers crossing the border (or
similar scenario). When the officer starts the interview process
only respond *"como"* or *"no English".* As he continues talking or
giving directions turn to your partner and say *"Vamos a matar a
este cerdo".* See how the interviewing cadet responds. If they do
nothing, ask *"What should you do?"* Involve the others in the
class if they seem to have no idea.

If the student does not speak decent Spanish, they will not
know what you are saying or what their reaction should be. If no
one responds with any ideas, ask if they are afraid for their
safety. If not, begin to make a flanking maneuver beside the
interviewing officer and look down at his gun. See if his reaction
changes from before. Look back to your accomplice and make the
same statement as before. Ask the officer if they feel uneasy at
this point and if they should react in some way or just keep
talking.

Advise the class that you just told your accomplice *"Let's kill
this pig."* Ask the class if it's important to understand some basic
Spanish since 45 million Americans speak it as their primary
language. Remind them that English is not the official language of
the United States. The fact is we do not have one because we are
a nation of immigrants.

If the officer cannot understand the language used by a group
of *suspects,* they should never let them speak to each other in

such a circumstance. Ever! It shows young officers the value of watching and understanding a person's body language for pre-attack indicators like *Pushing the Hair*.

Finish by showing the video of Constable Darrell Lunsford who was murdered in a similar manner. The cop killers not only spoke in Spanish just before the attack but also made overt indications that they were about to assault the constable. One man exited the car and then took his hat off indicating he was planning the assault. You may choose to take a hat off during one of your scenarios to see if cadets pick up on the indicator.

Partner Shot

You make a traffic stop for speeding. As you and your partner approach the car, the driver jumps out and shoots your partner who collapses in the roadway. Before you can return fire, the suspect runs off into a wooded area. What should you do? You can use this as a classroom scenario or role-play during *Stops & Approaches* training.

Did the cadets stay with the wounded officer or run after the suspect? Ask them why? It forces cadets to make a value judgment. If they follow the suspect into the woods, ask them what will happen to their partner left lying in the roadway. Should his medical attention and safety come first?

See how they defend their choices, and use them as a key point for a group discussion. Thinking through the choices at hand will create an atmosphere in which they become fully engaged with the learning process.

Do not give them your opinion on the scenario until they have discussed the topic thoroughly. Explain how adrenaline can cause a good cop to make a bad decision. Discussing these scenarios can keep our cadets from making the same mistakes as others before them.

Knife Attack

I have used this quick activity for *Foot Patrol, Stops & Approaches, Building Searches,* and *Prisoner Booking & Handling.*

Have a student quietly place a rubber (never real) knife in their pocket during a break. After everyone returns, start interviewing the student about a theft of which they are a suspect. Be the overzealous jerk cop who is rude and obnoxious to everyone and fails to use good officer safety skills. Give the signal (an offensive name or racial slur), and the audience will be in for a quick shock as the student stabs you. It will pull them into the presentation and you will have their attention while you explain what *rapidly evolving situations* look like. The role-play will show the importance of paying attention to their surroundings and keeping a safe stance during any interview.

Ask them: Could this happen to you if someone feels disrespected in front of other people on the street? Is it ever okay to use racial slurs towards a citizen? How close should you be when conducting an interview with a suspect on the street? How should you stand to protect yourself in the case of an unprovoked attack? How quick can an attack happen?

You Have 3 Seconds

Pull a student aside during a break and coach him on the following role-play. When the cadets are settled back in their seats, grab the volunteer in your arms and hold a rubber (never real) gun to their head. Have the student cry for the cadets to help them. Tell them, "You have three seconds to get out of here or I'm going to kill this kid." Start counting slowly "3-2-1." Have the volunteer plead with them to leave the class for his sake. Some will completely freeze up, others will leave the room, and a rare few will simulate shooting at you. Even in a classroom setting you can give them a shot of anxiety with this role-play. Discuss all the possible options available to them and ask why they chose a particular action or none at all.

The scenario is good to use at the beginning of the *Use of Force* topic to generate interest, and it works well with many other topics as a point of discussion.

Decision making is important and it forces students to consider the reality of using deadly force. Students realize they must understand the legal requirements *now* because there will not be time once they are confronted with a situation on the street.

Police Instructor Resources

The following are resources that can aid you in your duties as a police instructor; more links and resources are available at *LEOtrainer.com/links*. They will offer you new and improved *Ninja Instructor Skills* that are sure to enhance your training *mojo*.

ILEETA.org

The International Law Enforcement Educators and Trainers Association was formed in 2002 to serve the needs of criminal justice trainers and educators throughout the world. ILEETA provides information, training resources, member discounts and networking along with several law enforcement magazine subscriptions and quarterly publications. They also offer a highly recommended training conference each year. It is definitely worth your investment to join. The membership application is available at *LEOtrainer.com/ileeta*.

ILEETA is part of the *Phalanx LE* style. I consider my membership with the organization to be one of my best investments as a police instructor.

NLEARN.org

The National Law Enforcement Academy Resource Network links all the U.S. law enforcement training academies together and provides a variety of resources for commanders and instructors. They have a newsletter and public forums filled with valuable information for anyone who trains law enforcers. The organization is federally funded and free of charge.

Prezi.com

Prezi is the next generation of presentation design. It can incorporate your current PowerPoint slides into a new Prezi show that will wow any group you're training. And I mean any group! Prezi is the biggest advancement in presentation design since the slide format was developed decades ago, and the change is dramatic for instructors and their audience. The law enforcement audience you serve will love Prezi shows as a refreshing change of pace from the static slide shows they are familiar with. Prezi is a *Ninja instructor skill.*

Prezi lets you bring your ideas into one space and see how they relate helping you connect with your audience. Zoom out to see the big picture and zoom in to see details — a method you just have to see to fully understand. You can visit Prezi.com and use the software for free to see how you like it, and you will like it.

California POST post.ca.gov

California's Commission on Peace Officer Standards and Training is a great resource for instructors whether you are from California or not. They have publication and training resources that will benefit you and your students. If you visit their Instructor Development Institute website at www.postidi.com, you will see the dedication they have to our craft. It is second to none, and that is coming from a *Buckeye!*

TheIACP.org

The International Association of Chiefs of Police is a great resource for you as a police instructor. Their leadership and professionalism in the field of police training assures you that their resources are top notch. Police Chief Magazine is viewable online and is packed full of wisdom and ideas for your next class.

TrainingMag.com

Training magazine covers all the training issues that concern the business world, but the topics also apply to law enforcement educators as well. Their magazine and newsletters are filled with valuable information to enhance your presentation skills and are available online at no cost.

TED.com

TED is a nonprofit organization devoted to *Ideas Worth Spreading.* It started out in 1984 as a conference bringing together people from three worlds: Technology, Entertainment, and Design. Since then its scope has become broader. The site is filled with videos for you to pick up new ideas and presentation skills. If there is new technology connected to training and presentations, you will see it used first by a TED presenter.

FLETC.gov/legal

The Federal Law Enforcement Training Center is your best spot to find up-to-date legal resources. The cadre at the FLETC is second to none when it comes to staying on top of new case law. They have a monthly newsletter covering rulings from the U.S. Supreme Court and the Federal Circuit Courts of Appeal. You can download their *Legal Reference Book* that will answer just about any question you can think of regarding *Search & Seizure, Use of Force,* or *Miranda.*

LinkedIn.com Law Enforcement Training Groups

LinkedIn is a social networking site that was launched in 2003, mainly used by professionals. As of March 2011, LinkedIn reports more than 120 million registered users spanning more than 196 countries and territories worldwide. The network has hundreds of groups dedicated to law enforcement, training, and education that can benefit you. Join today and you will be able to network with instructors from around the corner or around the globe. The groups are listed at *LEOtrainer.com/forums.*

Slideshare.net

Slideshare is the YouTube of slide shows. The website has become host to a large number of educational and entertaining presentations. The site also supports a social web conferencing system which allows presenters to broadcast an audio and video feed while driving the slide show through the Internet. Slideshare can be an educational source for instructors to enhance their own skills and a tool to deliver training to any officer with an Internet connection.

History.com/this-day-in-history

Find interesting information concerning any day in history, and use it as an interesting way to open your next speech.

SPIM Factoid

When SPIM goes out in public (without his super suit), he wears a cowboy hat and moustache as a disguise. His secret identity is a peaceful man named Chuck Norris.

True Story!

 **My** Notes Ideas Cases Stories

About the Author

Richard lives on a farm in southwestern Ohio with his wife Gloria (below). Their daughter, Nadia (right), attends The Ohio State University and has served as a missionary in Mexico, Uganda, and Kenya. Their son, Richard Jr. (right), also attends The Ohio State University and serves in the U.S. Army as an Infantryman.

Currently, Richard instructs for several of Ohio's basic peace officer training academies and conducts advanced training for veteran law enforcers. He also serves on a team of investigators that reviews unresolved cases involving missing children.

Richard served as a patrol officer, criminal investigator, field training officer, police instructor, crime scene investigator, and school resource officer before retiring from a distinguished career in law enforcement. He has conducted training for officers, cadets, parents, and children and has presented in front of civic groups, governors, and White House cabinet members. He has developed prevention programs, designed workshops, and directed conferences.

Richard wrote this book to stimulate ideas, stories, discussions, and positive action by police instructors – he is committed to the advancement of law enforcement training.

"Blessed are the peacemakers, for they will be called children of God." ~Matthew 5:9

A Prayer for Law Enforcers

Heavenly father, protect me as a guardian of Your justice and mercy, that I may overcome evil and restore peace in the world.

Bestow upon me the courage to face the troubles of our society as a source of comfort and strength.

Inspire me to become an instrument of peace and a ray of hope to those who are hurting.

Strengthen my resolve that I may show bravery in the midst of evil, compassion to those in need, and integrity in everything I do.

Finally, I pray for You to watch over my family as I faithfully serve our society.

~Amen

24976642R00143

Made in the USA
Lexington, KY
13 August 2013